MISTY

IN LIGHT AND SHADE

Twenty-One Designs
By
Kim Hargreaves

CREDITS

DESIGNS & STYLING — *Kim Hargreaves*

EDITOR — *Kathleen Hargreaves*

MODEL — *Hannah Wright*

HAIR & MAKE-UP — *Diana Fisher*

PHOTOGRAPHY & EDITORIAL DESIGN — *Graham Watts*

LAYOUTS — *Angela Lin*

PATTERNS — *Sue Whiting & Trisha McKenzie*

First published in 2010 by Kim Hargreaves
Intake Cottage, 26 Underbank Old Road, Holmfirth
West Yorkshire, HD9 1EA, England
Reprinted in 2011

British Library Cataloguing in Publication Data
A catalogue record for this book is available from the British Library

ISBN–10   1–906487–07–2
ISBN–13   978–1–906487–07–2

CONTENTS

IN LIGHT AND SHADE

Awaken the senses. Take pleasure in daydreams of hazy meadows, the soft scent of wild flowers and the feel of summer's soft breeze, whilst cool cottons in calm shades enhance the tranquil mood.

Haze – *Sweater with generous neckline & deep raglans*

Arielle – *Pretty button through sweater with lace paneling*

Adore – Airy scarf edged with garter stitch

Fleeting – An understated Sloppy Joe

Fleeting – *An understated Sloppy Joe*

Bud – Long-line Boyfriend cardigan with basket weave trim

Blossom – *Sculptured peplum cardigan with nipped in waist*

Carrie – *Textured cardigan with collar & cording*

Lily – Close-fitting shrug with single button & garter stitch trim

Jess – *Waistcoat with an elegant drape & soft shawl collar*

Sage – A-line cardigan with cable & lace paneling

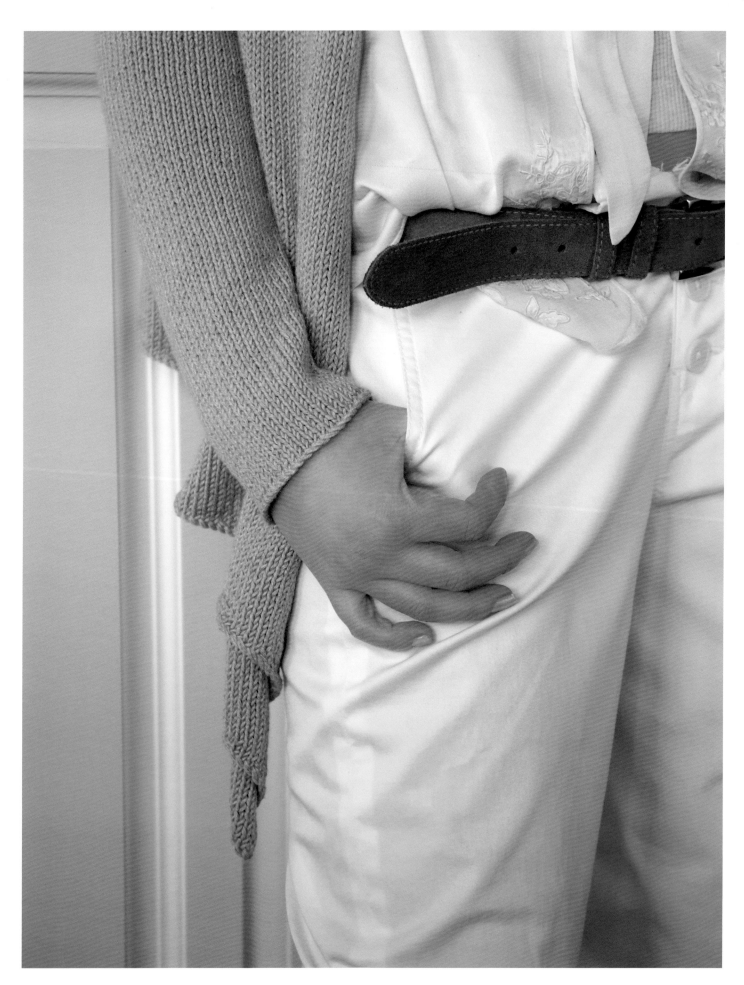

Embrace – Relaxed cardigan with draped fronts

Starr – *Slouchy hat worked in cables & lace panelling*

Lucy – *Textured jacket with covered buttons & crochet edgings*

Chalk – Relaxed belted wrap cardigan with moss stitch trim

Bud – *Boyfriend cardigan with basket weave trim*

Down – *Light as a feather sweater*

Peace – Neat fitting cardigan with textured yoke detail

Shimmer – Boxy cardigan worked in an open fabric

Anaïs – *Cropped cardigan worked in a lacy rib*

Cheer – Close fitting hat with rib & eyelet texture

Cloud – *Openwork crochet wrap*

Petal – Sweet sweater with texture & button trim

SUN
BEAMS
AND
DAY
DREAMS

ANAÏS

Lace cardigan with short sleeves

Recommendation

Suitable for the knitter with a little experience
Please see pages 42, 43 & 44 for photographs.

	XS	S	M	L	XL	XXL	
To fit bust	**81**	**86**	**91**	**97**	**102**	**109**	**cm**
	32	34	36	38	40	43	in

Rowan Milk Cotton DK

| | 5 | 6 | 6 | 7 | 7 | 8 | x 50gm |

Photographed in Pastille

Needles

1 pair 2¾mm (no 12) (US 2) needles
1 pair 3¼mm (no 10) (US 3) needles

Buttons – 10 (10: 10: 10: 11: 11)

Tension

26 sts and 31½ rows to 10 cm measured over
pattern using 3¼mm (US 3) needles.

BACK

Cast on 90 (98: 104: 110: 116: 128) sts
using 2¾mm (US 2) needles.
Row 1 (RS): K1 (2: 2: 2: 2: 2), *P1, K2, rep
from * to last 2 (0: 0: 0: 0: 0) sts, (P1, K1)
1 (0: 0: 0: 0: 0) times.
Row 2: P1 (2: 2: 2: 2: 2), *K1, P2, rep from *
to last 2 (0: 0: 0: 0: 0) sts, (K1, P1) 1 (0: 0:
0: 0: 0) times.
These 2 rows form rib.
Work in rib for a further 18 rows, ending
with a WS row.
Change to 3¼mm (US 3) needles.
Now work in patt as folls:
Row 1 (RS): K1 (0: 2: 0: 2: 2), P1 (0: 1: 0:
1: 1), *K2, P1, K2tog, yfrn, P1, rep from * to
last 4 (2: 5: 2: 5: 5) sts, K2, P1 (0: 1: 0: 1: 1),
K1 (0: 2: 0: 2: 2).
Row 2: P1 (2: 2: 2: 2: 2), *K1, P2, rep from *
to last 2 (0: 0: 0: 0: 0) sts, (K1, P1) 1 (0: 0:
0: 0: 0) times.
Row 3: K1 (0: 2: 0: 2: 2), P1 (0: 1: 0: 1: 1),
*K2, P1, yon, K2tog tbl, P1, rep from * to
last 4 (2: 5: 2: 5: 5) sts, K2, P1 (0: 1: 0: 1: 1),
K1 (0: 2: 0: 2: 2).
Row 4: As row 2.
These 4 rows form patt.
Cont in patt, shaping side seams by inc
1 st at each end of next and 3 foll 12th rows,
taking inc sts into patt.
98 (106: 112: 118: 124: 136) sts.
Work a further 9 (9: 11: 11: 11: 11) rows,
ending with a WS row.
(Back should measure 22 (22: 23: 23:
23: 23) cm.)
Shape armholes
Keeping patt correct, cast off 3 (4: 4: 5: 5: 6)
sts at beg of next 2 rows.
92 (98: 104: 108: 114: 124) sts.
Dec 1 st at each end of next 3 (5: 5: 7: 7: 9)
rows, then on foll 2 (2: 4: 2: 4: 6) alt rows.
82 (84: 86: 90: 92: 94) sts.
Work a further 45 (45: 41: 47: 47: 43)
rows, ending with a WS row.
(Armhole should measure 17 (18: 18:
19: 20: 21) cm.)

Shape shoulders and back neck

Next row (RS): Cast off 4 (4: 4: 5: 5: 6) sts,
patt until there are 8 (8: 9: 9: 10: 10) sts
on right needle and turn, leaving rem sts
on a holder.
Work each side of neck separately.
Cast off 4 sts at beg of next row.
Cast off rem 4 (4: 5: 5: 6: 6) sts.
With RS facing, rejoin yarn to rem sts, cast off
centre 58 (60: 60: 62: 62: 62) sts, patt to end.
Complete to match first side, reversing
shapings.

LEFT FRONT

Cast on 50 (54: 57: 60: 63: 69) sts using
2¾mm (US 2) needles.
Row 1 (RS): K1 (2: 2: 2: 2: 2), *P1, K2, rep
from * to last 7 sts, P7.
Row 2: K6, *K1, P2, rep from * to last 2 (0: 0:
0: 0: 0) sts, (K1, P1) 1 (0: 0: 0: 0: 0) times.
Row 3: K1 (2: 2: 2: 2: 2), *P1, K2, rep from *
to last 7 sts, P1, K6.
Row 4: P6, *K1, P2, rep from * to last 2 (0: 0:
0: 0: 0) sts, (K1, P1) 1 (0: 0: 0: 0: 0) times.
These 4 rows set the sts – front opening edge
6 sts in ridge patt with all other sts in rib.
Cont as set for a further 16 rows, ending with
a WS row.
Change to 3¼mm (US 3) needles.
Now work in patt as folls:
Row 1 (RS): K1 (0: 2: 0: 2: 2), P1 (0: 1: 0: 1:
1), *K2, P1, K2tog, yfrn, P1, rep from * to last
6 sts, P6.
Row 2: K6, *K1, P2, rep from * to last 2 (0: 0:
0: 0: 0) sts, (K1, P1) 1 (0: 0: 0: 0: 0) times.
Row 3: K1 (0: 2: 0: 2: 2), P1 (0: 1: 0: 1: 1),
*K2, P1, yon, K2tog tbl, P1, rep from * to last
6 sts, K6.
Row 4: P6, *K1, P2, rep from * to last 2 (0: 0:
0: 0: 0) sts, (K1, P1) 1 (0: 0: 0: 0: 0) times.
These 4 rows form patt.
Cont in patt, shaping side seam by inc 1 st at
beg of next and 3 foll 12th rows, taking inc sts
into patt. 54 (58: 61: 64: 67: 73) sts.
Work a further 9 (9: 11: 11: 11: 11) rows,
ending with a WS row.

Shape armhole

Keeping patt correct, cast off 3 (4: 4: 5: 5: 6) sts at beg of next row.
51 (54: 57: 59: 62: 67) sts.
Work 1 row.
Dec 1 st at armhole edge of next 3 (5: 5: 7: 7: 9) rows, then on foll 2 (2: 4: 2: 4: 6) alt rows.
46 (47: 48: 50: 51: 52) sts.
Work a further 21 (19: 13: 19: 19: 15) rows, ending after patt row 2 and with a WS row.

Shape neck

Next row (RS): Patt 22 (23: 25: 26: 27: 28) sts and turn, leaving rem 24 (24: 23: 24: 24: 24) sts on a holder.
Keeping patt correct, dec 1 st at neck edge of next 10 rows, then on foll 2 (3: 4: 4: 4: 4) alt rows, then on 2 foll 4th rows.
8 (8: 9: 10: 11: 12) sts.
Work 1 row, ending with a WS row.

Shape shoulder

Cast off 4 (4: 4: 5: 5: 6) sts at beg of next row.
Work 1 row.
Cast off rem 4 (4: 5: 5: 6: 6) sts.

RIGHT FRONT

Cast on 50 (54: 57: 60: 63: 69) sts using 2¾mm (US 2) needles.
Row 1 (RS): P6, *P1, K2, rep from * to last 2 (0: 0: 0: 0: 0) sts, (P1, K1) 1 (0: 0: 0: 0: 0) times.
Row 2: P1 (2: 2: 2: 2: 2), *K1, P2, rep from * to last 7 sts, K7.
Row 3 (buttonhole row): K2, K2tog tbl, yfwd (to make first buttonhole), K2, *P1, K2, rep from * to last 2 (0: 0: 0: 0: 0) sts, (P1, K1) 1 (0: 0: 0: 0: 0) times.
Row 4: P1 (2: 2: 2: 2: 2), *K1, P2, rep from * to last 7 sts, K1, P6.
These 4 rows set the sts – front opening edge 6 sts in ridge patt with all other sts in rib.
Cont as set for a further 16 rows, making buttonholes as set by row 3 in 7th and 15th (15th: 15th: 0: 15th: 15th) of these rows and ending with a WS row.
(3 (3: 3: 2: 3: 3) buttonholes completed.)
Change to 3¼mm (US 3) needles.
Now work in patt as folls:
Row 1 (RS): P7, K2tog, yfrn, P1, *K2, P1, K2tog, yfrn, P1, rep from * to last 4 (2: 5: 2: 5: 5) sts, K2, P1 (0: 1: 0: 1: 1), K1 (0: 2: 0: 2: 2).
Row 2: P1 (2: 2: 2: 2: 2), *K1, P2, rep from * to last 7 sts, K7.

Row 3: K6 (6: 6: 2: 6: 6), (K2tog tbl, yfwd - to make 3rd buttonhole, K2) 0 (0: 0: 1: 0: 0) times, P1, yon, K2tog tbl, P1, *K2, P1, yon, K2tog tbl, P1, rep from * to last 4 (2: 5: 2: 5: 5) sts, K2, P1 (0: 1: 0: 1: 1), K1 (0: 2: 0: 2: 2).
Row 4: P1 (2: 2: 2: 2: 2), *K1, P2, rep from * to last 7 sts, K1, P6.
These 4 rows form patt. (3 buttonholes completed.)
Making a further 6 (6: 6: 6: 7: 7) buttonholes in 7th (7th: 7th: 11th: 7th: 9th) and every foll 12th row, complete to match left front, reversing shaping and working first row of neck shapings as folls:

Shape neck

Next row (RS): K2, K2tog tbl, yfwd (to make last buttonhole), patt 20 (20: 19: 20: 20: 20) sts and slip these 24 (24: 23: 24: 24: 24) sts onto a holder, patt to end.
22 (23: 25: 26: 27: 28) sts.

SLEEVES (both alike)

Cast on 74 (78: 78: 82: 84: 88) sts using 2¾mm (US 2) needles.
Row 1 (RS): K2 (1: 1: 0: 1: 0), *P1, K2, rep from * to last 0 (2: 2: 1: 2: 1) sts, P0 (1: 1: 1: 1: 1), K0 (1: 1: 0: 1: 0).
Row 2: P2 (1: 1: 0: 1: 0), *K1, P2, rep from * to last 0 (2: 2: 1: 2: 1) sts, K0 (1: 1: 1: 1: 1), P0 (1: 1: 0: 1: 0).
These 2 rows form rib.
Work in rib for a further 8 rows, ending with a WS row.
Change to 3¼mm (US 3) needles.
Now work in patt as folls:
Row 1 (RS): K0 (1: 1: 0: 1: 0), P0 (1: 1: 1: 1: 1), (K2tog, yfrn, P1) 0 (0: 0: 1: 1: 0) times, *K2, P1, K2tog, yfrn, P1, rep from * to last 2 (4: 4: 0: 1: 3) sts, K2 (2: 2: 0: 1: 2), P0 (1: 1: 0: 0: 1), K0 (1: 1: 0: 0: 0).
Row 2: P2 (1: 1: 0: 1: 0), *K1, P2, rep from * to last 0 (2: 2: 1: 2: 1) sts, K0 (1: 1: 1: 1: 1), P0 (1: 1: 0: 1: 0).
These 2 rows set position of patt as given for back.
Cont in patt for a further 0 (0: 0: 4: 4: 6) rows, ending with a WS row. (Sleeve should measure 4 (4: 4: 5: 5: 6) cm.)

Shape top

Keeping patt correct, cast off 3 (4: 4: 5: 5: 6) sts at beg of next 2 rows.
68 (70: 70: 72: 74: 76) sts.

Dec 1 st at each end of next 3 rows, then on foll alt row, then on 4 foll 4th rows.
52 (54: 54: 56: 58: 60) sts.
Work 1 row.
Dec 1 st at each end of next and every foll alt row to 42 sts, then on foll 5 rows, ending with a WS row.
Cast off rem 32 sts.

MAKING UP

Pin the pieces out and steam gently without allowing the iron to touch the yarn.
Join both shoulder seams using back stitch or mattress stitch if preferred.

Neckband

With RS facing and using 2¾mm (US 2) needles, slip 24 (24: 23: 24: 24: 24) sts from right front holder onto right needle, rejoin yarn and pick up and knit 24 (26: 28: 28: 28: 28) sts up right side of neck, 64 (66: 67: 68: 68: 68) sts from back, and 24 (26: 28: 28: 28: 28) sts down left side of neck, then patt 24 (24: 23: 24: 24: 24) sts from left front holder.
160 (166: 169: 172: 172: 172) sts.
Row 1 (WS): Patt 6 sts, K1, *P2, K1, rep from * to last 6 sts, patt 6 sts.
Row 2: Patt 6 sts, P1, *K2, P1, rep from * to last 6 sts, patt 6 sts.
These 2 rows set the sts – front opening edge 6 sts still in patt with all other sts in rib.
Cont as set for a further 4 rows, ending with a RS row.
Cast off in patt (on WS).
Join side seams. Join sleeve seams. Insert sleeves into armholes. Sew on buttons.

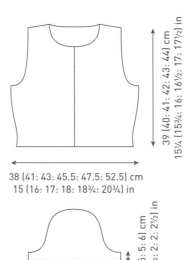

38 (41: 43: 45.5: 47.5: 52.5) cm
15 (16: 17: 18: 18¾: 20¾) in

39 (40: 41: 42: 43: 44) cm
15¼ (15¾: 16: 16½: 17: 17½) in

4 (4: 4: 5: 5: 6) cm
1½ (1½: 1½: 2: 2: 2½) in

HAZE

Sweater with generous neckline & deep raglans

Recommendation

Suitable for the knitter with a little experience
Please see pages 7, 8 & 9 for photographs.

	XS	S	M	L	XL	XXL	
To fit bust	81	86	91	97	102	109	cm
	32	34	36	38	40	43	in

Rowan Pima Cotton

10	11	11	12	12	13	x 50gm	

Photographed in Badger

Needles

1 pair 3mm (no 11) (US 2/3) needles
1 pair 3¾mm (no 9) (US 5) needles

Tension

23 sts and 30 rows to 10 cm measured over
stocking stitch using 3¾mm (US 5) needles.

BACK

Lower border

Cast on 36 sts using 3mm (US 2/3) needles.
Row 1 (RS): Purl.
Row 2: Knit.
Row 3: K12, wrap next st (by slipping next st
from left needle to right needle, taking yarn
to opposite side of work between needles and
then slipping same st back onto left needle –
when working across wrapped sts, work the
wrapped st and the wrapping loop tog as one
st) and turn.
Row 4: Purl.
Row 5: P24, wrap next st and turn.
Row 6: Knit.
These 6 rows complete side seam shaping.
Now work in border patt as folls:
Row 1 (RS): Knit.
Rows 2 and 3: Purl.
Rows 4 and 5: Knit.
Row 6: P2, *yrn, P2tog, rep from * to end.
Row 7: Purl.
Rows 8 and 9: Knit.
Rows 10 and 11: Purl.
Row 12: Knit.
These 12 rows form border patt.
Rep last 12 rows 8 (9: 10: 10: 11: 12) times
more, then rows 1 to 10 again, ending with
a WS row.
Next row (RS): P24, wrap next st and turn.
Next row: Knit.
Next row: K12, wrap next st and turn.
Next row: Purl.
Next row: Purl.
Next row: Knit.
Cast off.

Main section

With RS facing and using 3mm (US 2/3)
needles, pick up and knit 97 (103: 109: 115:
121: 129) sts evenly along shorter row-end
edge of lower border.
Change to 3¾mm (US 5) needles.
Beg with a P row, work in st st for 11 rows,
ending with a WS row.
Next row (inc) (RS): K3, M1, K to last 3 sts,
M1, K3.

Working all side seam increases as set by last
row, inc 1 st at each end of 10th and foll 10th
row, then on 2 foll 8th rows, then on foll 6th
row. 109 (115: 121: 127: 133: 141) sts.
Cont straight until back measures 20 (20: 21:
21: 21: 21) cm **from pick-up row,** ending with
a WS row.

Shape raglan armholes

Cast off 8 sts at beg of next 2 rows.
93 (99: 105: 111: 117: 125) sts.
Work 4 (4: 4: 2: 0: 0) rows.
Next row (RS): K1, K2tog, patt to last 3 sts,
K2tog tbl, K1.
Working all decreases as set by last row, dec 1
st at each end of 6th (6th: 6th: 4th: 2nd: 2nd)
and foll 0 (0: 0: 0: 2: 9) alt rows, then on 9 (7:
1: 0: 0: 0) foll 6th rows, then on 4 (8: 17: 20:
21: 18) foll 4th rows.
63 (65: 65: 67: 67: 67) sts.
Work 1 row, ending with a WS row.
Cast off.

FRONT

Work as given for back until 71 (73: 73: 75:
75: 75) sts rem in raglan armhole shaping.
Work 3 rows, ending with a WS row.

Shape neck

Next row (RS): K1, K2tog, K10 and turn,
leaving rem sts on a holder.
Work each side of neck separately.
Cast off 4 sts at beg of next row, then 3 sts
at beg of foll alt row. 5 sts.
Next row (RS): K1, K2tog, K2. 4 sts.
Dec 1 st at neck edge of next 3 rows, ending
with a WS row.
Fasten off rem 1 st.
With RS facing, rejoin yarn to rem sts, cast
off centre 45 (47: 47: 49: 49: 49) sts, K to
last 3 sts, K2tog tbl, K1. 12 sts.
Complete to match first side, reversing
shapings.

SLEEVES (both alike)

Cuff border

Cast on 20 sts using 3mm (US 2/3) needles.
Row 1 (RS): Purl.

54

Row 2: Knit.

Row 3: K7, wrap next st and turn.

Row 4: Purl.

Row 5: P14, wrap next st and turn.

Row 6: Knit.

These 6 rows complete side shaping.

Beg with patt row 5, now work in border patt as given for lower border of back for 66 (66: 66: 78: 78: 78) rows, ending after patt row 10 and with a WS row.

Next row (RS): P14, wrap next st and turn.

Next row: Knit.

Next row: K7, wrap next st and turn.

Next row: Purl.

Next row: Purl.

Next row: Knit.

Cast off.

Main section

With RS facing and using 3mm (US 2/3) needles, pick up and knit 75 (75: 77: 79: 79: 81) sts evenly along **longer** row-end edge of cuff border.

Change to 3¾mm (US 5) needles.

Working all increases in same way as side seam increases and beg with a P row, work in st st, shaping sides by inc 1 st at each end of 4th and 13 (13: 15: 16: 17: 18) foll 4th rows, then on foll 10 (11: 9: 8: 8: 7) alt rows.

123 (125: 127: 129: 131: 133) sts.

Work 1 row, ending with a WS row. (Sleeve should measure 26 (27: 28: 29: 30: 31) cm **from pick-up row.**)

Shape raglan

Cast off 8 sts at beg of next 2 rows.

107 (109: 111: 113: 115: 117) sts.

Next row (RS): K1, K2tog, K to last 3 sts, K2tog tbl, K1.

Next row: (P1, P2tog tbl) 1 (0: 1: 1: 0: 0) times, P to last 3 (0: 3: 3: 0: 0) sts, (P2tog, P1) 1 (0: 1: 1: 0: 0) times.

103 (107: 107: 109: 113: 115) sts.

Working all decreases as set by first of last 2 rows, dec 1 st at each end of next and every foll alt row until 29 sts rem.

Work 1 row, ending with a WS row.

Left sleeve only

Dec 1 st at each end of next row, then cast off 6 sts at beg of foll row. 21 sts.

Dec 1 st at beg of next row, then cast off 6 sts at beg of foll row. 14 sts.

Right sleeve only

Cast off 7 sts at beg and dec 1 st at end of next row. 21 sts.

Work 1 row.

Cast off 6 sts at beg and dec 1 st at end of next row. 14 sts.

Work 1 row.

Both sleeves

Rep last 2 rows once more.

Cast off rem 7 sts.

MAKING UP

Pin the pieces out and steam gently without allowing the iron to touch the yarn.

Join both front and right back raglan seams using back stitch or mattress stitch if preferred.

Neckband

With RS facing and using 3mm (US 2/3) needles, pick up and knit 23 sts from top of left sleeve, 10 sts down left side of neck, 45 (47: 47: 49: 49: 49) sts from front, 10 sts up right side of neck, 23 sts from top of right sleeve, then 61 (63: 63: 65: 65: 65) sts from back. 172 (176: 176: 180: 180: 180) sts.

Beg with a K row, work in rev st st for 4 rows, ending with a **RS** row. Cast off knitwise (on **WS**).

Join left back raglan and neckband seam. Join side and sleeve seams.

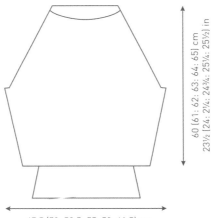

60 (61: 62: 63: 64: 65) cm
23½ (24: 24½: 24¾: 25¼: 25½) in

47.5 (50: 52.5: 55: 58: 61.5) cm
18¾ (19¾: 20¾: 21¾: 22¾: 24¼) in

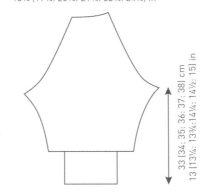

33 (34: 35: 36: 37: 38) cm
13 (13¼: 13¾: 14¼: 14½: 15) in

ARIELLE

Pretty button through sweater

Recommendation

Suitable for the knitter with a little experience
Please see pages 10 & 11 for photographs.

	XS	S	M	L	XL	XXL	
To fit bust	81	86	91	97	102	109	cm
	32	34	36	38	40	43	in

Rowan Fine Milk Cotton

| | 6 | 6 | 7 | 7 | 8 | 9 | x 50gm |

Photographed in Opaque

Needles

1 pair 2¼mm (no 13) (US 1) needles
1 pair 2¾mm (no 12) (US 2) needles

Buttons – 9

Tension

29 sts and 38 rows to 10 cm measured over
main pattern using 2¾mm (US 2) needles.

Pattern note: The number of sts varies whilst
working main patt. Do NOT count sts after
patt rows 1 or 2. The st counts given do NOT
include the extra sts made whilst working patt
and presume each patt panel has 13 sts at all
times.

BACK

Lower border

Cast on 20 (23: 23: 26: 26: 26) sts using
2¼mm (US 1) needles.
Now work in border patt as folls:
Row 1 (WS): Knit.
Row 2: P to last 3 sts, wrap next st (by
slipping next st on left needle onto right
needle, taking yarn to opposite side of work
between needles and then slipping same st
back onto left needle – when working back
across wrapped sts, work the wrapped st and
the wrapping loop tog as one st) and turn.
Row 3: Knit.
Row 4: P to last 3 sts, K3.
Row 5: K3, P to end.
Row 6: (K2tog, yfwd) to last 6 (5: 5: 6: 6:6)
sts, K3 (2: 2: 3: 3: 3), wrap next st and turn.
Row 7: Purl.
Row 8: Knit.
These 8 rows form border patt.
Rep last 8 rows 34 (36: 39: 41: 43: 47) times
more, then rows 1 to 3 once more, ending with
a WS row.
Cast off purlwise (on RS) but do **NOT** fasten off.

Main section

With RS facing and using 2¾mm (US 2)
needles, pick up and knit 114 (120: 128: 136:
142: 154) sts evenly along shorter row-end
edge of lower border.
Next row (WS): Purl.
Now work in main patt as folls:
Row 1 (RS): K17 (19: 22: 25: 27: 33), *P1,
K1 tbl, P1, K2tog tbl, (yfwd, K1) 3 times, yfwd,
K2tog, P1, K1 tbl, P1*, K7 (7: 8: 8: 9: 9), rep
from * to * once more, K14 (16: 16: 18: 18:
18), rep from * to * once more, K7 (7: 8: 8: 9:
9), rep from * to * once more, K to end.
Row 2: P17 (19: 22: 25: 27: 33), *K1, P1 tbl,
K1, P9, K1, P1 tbl, K1*, P7 (7: 8: 8: 9: 9), rep
from * to * once more, P14 (16: 16: 18: 18:
18), rep from * to * once more, P7 (7: 8: 8: 9:
9), rep from * to * once more, P to end.
Row 3: K2, K2tog, K13 (15: 18: 21: 23: 29),
*P1, K1 tbl, P1, K2tog tbl, K5, K2tog, P1, K1
tbl, P1*, K7 (7: 8: 8: 9: 9), rep from * to * once

more, K14 (16: 16: 18: 18: 18), rep from * to
* once more, K7 (7: 8: 8: 9: 9), rep from * to *
once more, K to last 4 sts, K2tog tbl, K2.
112 (118: 126: 134: 140: 152) sts.
Row 4: P16 (18: 21: 24: 26: 32), *K1, P1 tbl,
K1, P7, K1, P1 tbl, K1*, P7 (7: 8: 8: 9: 9), rep
from * to * once more, P14 (16: 16: 18: 18:
18), rep from * to * once more, P7 (7: 8: 8: 9:
9), rep from * to * once more, P to end.
These 4 rows form main patt and beg side
seam shaping.
Working all side seam decreases as set by
row 3, cont in patt, shaping side seams by
dec 1 st at each end of 5th and foll 6th row,
then on 3 foll 4th rows.
102 (108: 116: 124: 130: 142) sts.**
Work 13 rows, ending with a WS row.
Next row (RS): K3, M1, patt to last 3 sts, M1, K3.
Working all side seam increases as set by last
row, inc 1 st at each end of 10th and 6 foll
10th rows. 118 (124: 132: 140: 146: 158) sts.
Work a further 11 (7: 11: 7: 7: 7) rows, ending
with a WS row. (Back should measure 32 (31:
32: 31: 31: 31) cm from main section
pick-up row.)

Shape armholes

Keeping patt correct, cast off 5 (6: 6: 7: 7: 8)
sts at beg of next 2 rows.
108 (112: 120: 126: 132: 142) sts.
Dec 1 st at each end of next 5 (5: 7: 7: 9: 11)
rows, then on foll 2 (3: 4: 5: 5: 6) alt rows,
then on foll 4th row.
92 (94: 96: 100: 102: 106) sts.
Work a further 49 (51: 47: 49: 51: 51) rows,
ending with a WS row. (Armhole should
measure 17 (18: 18: 19: 20: 21) cm.)
Shape shoulders and back neck
Cast off 7 (7: 7: 8: 8: 9) sts at beg of next
2 rows.
78 (80: 82: 84: 86: 88) sts.
Next row (RS): Cast off 7 (7: 7: 8: 8: 9) sts,
patt until there are 11 (11: 12: 11: 12: 12)
sts on right needle and turn, leaving rem
sts on a holder.
Work each side of neck separately.
Cast off 4 sts at beg of next row.

Cast off rem 7 (7: 8: 7: 8: 8) sts.
With RS facing, rejoin yarn to rem sts, cast off centre 42 (44: 44: 46: 46: 46) sts, patt to end.
Complete to match first side, reversing shapings.

FRONT

Work as given for back to **.
Work 3 (3: 7: 3: 7: 11) rows, ending with a WS row.
Divide for front opening
Next row (RS): Patt 48 (51: 55: 59: 62: 68) sts and turn, leaving rem sts on a holder.
Work each side of front separately.
Next row (WS): Cast on and K 6 sts, patt to end.
54 (57: 61: 65: 68: 74) sts.
Keeping patt correct, now work ridge patt over front opening edge 6 sts as folls:
Row 1 (RS): (K3, M1) 0 (0: 0: 0: 0: 1) times, patt to last 6 sts, K6.
Row 2: P6, patt to end.
Row 3: Patt to last 6 sts, P6.
Row 4: K6, patt to end.
These 4 rows form ridge patt over front opening edge 6 sts.
Working side seam increases as set by back, cont as now set, shaping side seam by inc 1 st at beg of 5th (5th: next: 5th: next: 7th) and 7 (7: 7: 7: 7: 6) foll 10th rows.
62 (65: 69: 73: 76: 82) sts.
Work a further 11 (7: 11: 7: 7: 7) rows, ending with a WS row.

Shape armhole

Keeping patt correct, cast off 5 (6: 6: 7: 7: 8) sts at beg of next row.
57 (59: 63: 66: 69: 74) sts.
Work 1 row.
Dec 1 st at armhole edge of next 5 (5: 7: 7: 9: 11) rows, then on foll 2 (3: 4: 5: 5: 6) alt rows, then on foll 4th row.
49 (50: 51: 53: 54: 56) sts.
Work a further 23 (25: 21: 19: 21: 21) rows, ending with a WS row.

Shape neck

Next row (RS): Patt 33 (33: 34: 36: 37: 39) sts and turn, leaving rem 16 (17: 17: 17: 17: 17) sts on another holder.
Keeping patt correct, dec 1 st at neck edge of next 6 rows, then on foll 4 alt rows, then on 2 (2: 2: 3: 3: 3) foll 4th rows.
21 (21: 22: 23: 24: 26) sts.
Work 3 rows, ending with a WS row.

Shape shoulder

Cast off 7 (7: 7: 8: 8: 9) sts at beg of next and foll alt row.
Work 1 row.
Cast off rem 7 (7: 8: 7: 8: 8) sts.
With RS facing, rejoin yarn to rem 54 (57: 61: 65: 68: 74) sts and cont as folls:
Row 1 (RS): P6, patt to end.
Row 2: Patt to last 6 sts, K6.
Row 3: K6, patt to last 0 (0: 0: 0: 0: 3) sts, (M1, K3) 0 (0: 0: 0: 0: 1) times.
Row 4: Patt to last 6 sts, P6.
These 4 rows form ridge patt over front opening edge 6 sts.
Keeping sts correct as now set, work 2 rows, ending with a WS row.
Next row (buttonhole row) (RS): K2, K2tog tbl, yfwd (to make a buttonhole), patt to last 0 (0: 3: 0: 3: 0) sts, (M1, K3) 0 (0: 1: 0: 1: 0) times.
Making a further 7 buttonholes in this way on every foll 16th row, complete to match first side, reversing shapings and working first row of neck shaping as folls:

Shape neck

Next row (RS): K2, K2tog tbl, yfwd (to make 9th buttonhole), patt 12 (13: 13: 13: 13: 13) sts and slip these 16 (17: 17: 17: 17: 17) sts onto another holder, patt to end.
33 (33: 34: 36: 37: 39) sts.

SLEEVES (both alike)

Cast on 8 sts using 2¾mm (US 2) needles.
Row 1 (RS): Purl.
Rows 2 and 3: Knit.
Row 4: Purl.
These 4 rows form ridge patt.
Cont in ridge patt, inc 1 st at end of 5th and 3 foll 4th rows, then on foll 7 alt rows, then on foll 4th row. 20 sts.
Work a further 49 (57: 57: 65: 73: 81) rows, ending with patt row 4 and a WS row.
Dec 1 st at end of next and foll 4th row, then on foll 7 alt rows, then on 3 foll 4th rows. 8 sts.
Work a further 7 rows, ending with patt row 2 and a WS row.
Cast off.

MAKING UP

Pin the pieces out and steam gently without allowing the iron to touch the yarn.
Join both shoulder seams using back stitch or mattress stitch if preferred.

Neckband

With RS facing and using 2¼mm (US 1) needles, slip 16 (17: 17: 17: 17: 17) sts from right front holder onto right needle, rejoin yarn and pick up and knit 30 (30: 30: 34: 34: 34) sts up right side of neck, 50 (52: 52: 54: 54: 54) sts from back, and 30 (30: 30: 34: 34: 34) sts down left side of neck, then patt 16 (17: 17: 17: 17: 17) sts from left front holder.
142 (146: 146: 156: 156: 156) sts.
Beg with a K row, work in rev st st for 6 rows, ending with a RS row.
Cast off knitwise (on **WS**).
Join side seams. Join sleeve seams. Insert sleeves into armholes. Sew cast-on edge of left front in place behind right front at base of front opening. Sew on buttons.

49 (49: 50: 50: 51: 52) cm
19¼ (19¼: 19¾: 19¾: 20: 20½) in

40.5 (43: 45.5: 48.5: 50.5: 54.5) cm
16 (17: 18: 19: 20: 21½) in

FLEETING

Sloppy joe

Recommendation

Suitable for the knitter with a little experience
Please see pages 13 & 14 for photographs.

	XS	S	M	L	XL	XXL	
To fit bust	**81**	**86**	**91**	**97**	**102**	**109**	cm
	32	34	36	38	40	43	in

Rowan Pima Cotton

12	12	13	13	14	15 x 50gm

Photographed in Millet

Needles

1 pair 3¼mm (no 10) (US 3) needles
1 pair 3¾mm (no 9) (US 5) needles

Tension

23 sts and 30 rows to 10 cm measured over
stocking stitch using 3¾mm (US 5) needles.

BACK

Cast on 136 (140: 148: 152: 160: 168) sts
using 3¼mm (US 3) needles.
Row 1 (RS): K1, P2, *K2, P2, rep from * to last
st, K1.
Row 2: P1, K2, *P2, K2, rep from * to last st, P1.
These 2 rows form rib.
Work in rib for a further 32 rows, dec 1 (0: 1:
0: 1: 1) st at each end of last row and ending
with a WS row.
134 (140: 146: 152: 158: 166) sts.
Place markers at both ends of last row.
Change to 3¾mm (US 5) needles.
Beg with a K row, work in st st until back
measures 58 (59: 60: 61: 62: 63) cm **from
markers,** ending with a WS row.

Shape shoulders

Cast off 3 (4: 4: 4: 4: 5) sts at beg of next
4 (18: 16: 12: 6: 18) rows, then 4 (0: 5: 5: 5:
0) sts at beg of foll 14 (0: 2: 6: 12: 0) rows.
66 (68: 72: 74: 74: 76) sts.

Shape back neck

Next row (RS): Cast off 4 (4: 5: 5: 5: 5) sts,
K until there are 8 (8: 9: 9: 9: 10) sts on right
needle and turn, leaving rem sts on a holder.
Work each side of neck separately.
Cast off 4 sts at beg of next row.
Cast off rem 4 (4: 5: 5: 5: 6) sts.
With RS facing, rejoin yarn to rem sts, cast off
centre 42 (44: 44: 46: 46: 46) sts, K to end.
Complete to match first side, reversing shapings.

FRONT

Cast on 136 (140: 148: 152: 160: 168) sts
using 3¼mm (US 3) needles.
Work in rib as given for back for 24 rows, dec
1 (0: 1: 0: 1: 1) st at each end of last row and
ending with a WS row.
134 (140: 146: 152: 158: 166) sts.
Place markers at both ends of last row.
Change to 3¾mm (US 5) needles.
Beg with a K row and measuring **from markers**
(as back is 10 rows longer than front), work in st
st until 16 (16: 16: 18: 18: 18) rows less have
been worked than on back to beg of shoulder
shaping, ending with a WS row.

Shape front neck

Next row (RS): K57 (59: 62: 65: 68: 72)
and turn, leaving rem sts on a holder.
Work each side of neck separately.
Dec 1 st at neck edge of next 8 rows, then
on foll 3 (3: 3: 4: 4: 4) alt rows.
46 (48: 51: 53: 56: 60) sts.
Work 1 row, ending with a WS row.

Shape shoulder

Cast off 3 (4: 4: 4: 4: 5) sts at beg of next and
foll 1 (9: 7: 5: 2: 9) alt rows, then 4 (0: 5: 5: 5:
0) sts at beg of foll 8 (0: 2: 4: 7: 0) alt rows,
and at the same time dec 1 st at neck edge
of next and foll alt row, then on 2 foll 4th rows.
Work 1 row.
Cast off rem 4 (4: 5: 5: 5: 6) sts.
With RS facing, rejoin yarn to rem sts, cast off
centre 20 (22: 22: 22: 22: 22) sts, K to end.
Complete to match first side, reversing shapings.

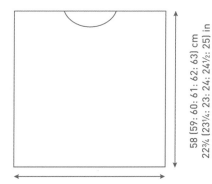

58 (59: 60: 61: 62: 63) cm
22¾ (23¼: 23: 24: 24½: 25) in

58.5 (61: 63.5: 66: 68.5: 72) cm
23 (24: 25: 26: 27: 28½) in

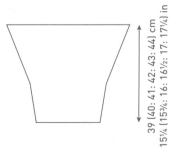

39 (40: 41: 42: 43: 44) cm
15¼ (15¾: 16: 16½: 17: 17¼) in

Continued on next page

ADORE
Pretty scarf

Recommendation
Suitable for the novice knitter
Please see pages 12 & 13 for photographs.

Rowan Kidsilk Haze
2 x 25gm
Photographed in Smoke

Needles
1 pair 5mm (no 6) (US 8) needles

Tension
16 sts and 20 rows to 10 cm measured over
pattern using 5mm (US 8) needles.

Finished size
Completed scarf measures approx 208 cm
(82 in) long and 31 cm (12¼ in) wide.

SCARF
Cast on 100 sts using 5mm (US 8) needles.
Row 1 (RS): *K2, lift 2nd st on right needle off
first st and off right needle, rep from * to end.
50 sts.
Row 2: Cast on 1 st, cast off 1 st, K until there
are 5 sts on right needle, *P2tog, yrn, rep from
* to last 5 sts, K5.
Rep last row until scarf measures approx 208
cm (or until there is sufficient yarn left to work
cast-off).
Cast off **loosely**.

Fleeting

SLEEVES (both alike)
Cast on 56 (56: 58: 60: 60: 62) sts using
3¼mm (US 3) needles.
Row 1 (RS): P1 (1: 0: 1: 1: 0), K2, *P2, K2, rep
from * to last 1 (1: 0: 1: 1: 0) st, P1 (1: 0: 1: 1: 0).
Row 2: K1 (1: 0: 1: 1: 0), P2, *K2, P2, rep
from * to last 1 (1: 0: 1: 1: 0) st, K1 (1: 0: 1:
1: 0).
These 2 rows form rib.
Cont in rib, shaping sides by inc 1 st at each
end of 5th and 2 foll 6th rows, taking inc sts
into rib.
62 (62: 64: 66: 66: 68) sts.
Work a further 5 rows, ending with a WS row.
(24 rows of rib completed.)
Change to 3¾mm (US 5) needles.

Next row (inc) (RS): K3, M1, K to last 3 sts,
M1, K3.
Working all sleeve increases as set by last row
and beg with a P row, cont in st st, shaping
sides by inc 1 st at each end of 6th and 4 (3:
5: 6: 6: 7) foll 6th rows, then on 15 (17: 15:
14: 15: 14) foll 4th rows. 104 (106: 108: 110:
112: 114) sts.
Work 3 rows, ending with a WS row. (Sleeve
should measure 39 (40: 41: 42: 43: 44) cm.)
Cast off.

MAKING UP
Pin the pieces out and steam gently without
allowing the iron to touch the yarn.
Join right shoulder seam using back stitch or
mattress stitch if preferred.

Neckband
With RS facing and using 3¼mm (US 3)
needles, pick up and knit 36 (36: 36: 38: 38:
38) sts down left side of neck, 20 (22: 22: 22:
22: 22) sts from front, 36 (36: 36: 38: 38: 38)
sts up right side of neck, then 50 (52: 52: 54:
54: 54) sts from back.
142 (146: 146: 152: 152: 152) sts.
Beg with a K row, work in rev st st for 4 rows,
ending with a **RS** row. Cast off knitwise (on **WS**).
Join left shoulder and neckband seam. Place
markers along side seam edges 22.5 (23:
23.5: 24: 24.5: 25) cm either side of shoulder
seams and sew sleeves to body between these
points. Join side and sleeve seams, leaving
side seams open below markers.

UD

...ic cardigan in two lengths

Recommendation

Suitable for the knitter with a little experience
Please see pages 15, 34 & 35 for photographs.

	XS	S	M	L	XL	XXL	
To fit bust	**81**	**86**	**91**	**97**	**102**	**109**	**cm**
	32	34	36	38	40	43	in

Rowan Summer Tweed

Shorter cardigan

      10 11 11 11 12 13 x 50gm

Longer cardigan

      11 12 12 12 13 14 x 50gm

Shorter cardigan photographed in Oats, and
longer cardigan photographed in Navy

Needles

1 pair 4mm (no 8) (US 6) needles
1 pair 5mm (no 6) (US 8) needles

Buttons – 4

Tension

16 sts and 23 rows to 10 cm measured over
reverse stocking stitch using 5mm (US 8)
needles.

...7 (81: 85: 89: 93: 99) sts using
...6) needles.

...1 (RS): P0 (0: 2: 0: 0: 0), K1 (3: 3: 1: 3:
0), *P3, K3, rep from * to last 4 (0: 2: 4: 0: 3)
sts, P3 (0: 2: 3: 0: 3), K1 (0: 0: 1: 0: 0).

Row 2: K0 (0: 2: 0: 0: 0), P1 (3: 3: 1: 3: 0),
*K3, P3, rep from * to last 4 (0: 2: 4: 0: 3) sts,
K3 (0: 2: 3: 0: 3), P1 (0: 0: 1: 0: 0).

Rows 3 and 4: As rows 1 and 2.

Row 5: As row 2.

Row 6: As row 1.

Rows 7 and 8: As rows 5 and 6.

These 8 rows form basket st patt.

Work in basket st patt for a further 12 (16: 16:
20: 20: 24) rows, ending with a WS row.

Change to 5mm (US 8) needles.

Beg with a P row, now work in rev st st as folls:

Shorter cardigan only

Cont straight until back measures 51 (52: 52:
53: 53: 54) cm, ending with a WS row.

Longer cardigan only

Cont straight until back measures 61 (62: 62:
63: 63: 64) cm, ending with a WS row.

Both cardigans

Shape armholes

Cast off 4 sts at beg of next 2 rows.

69 (73: 77: 81: 85: 91) sts.

Dec 1 st at each end of next 5 (5: 7: 7: 7: 9)
rows, then on foll 3 (4: 2: 3: 3: 3) alt rows,
then on foll 4th row.

51 (53: 57: 59: 63: 65) sts.

Cont straight until armhole measures 18 (18:
19: 19: 20: 20) cm, ending with a WS row.

Shape back neck

Next row (RS): P14 (15: 16: 17: 18: 19) and
turn, leaving rem sts on a holder.

Work each side of neck separately.

Dec 1 st at neck edge of next row.

13 (14: 15: 16: 17: 18) sts.

Shape shoulder

Cast off 4 (4: 5: 5: 5: 5) sts at beg of next row,
then 4 (4: 4: 5: 5: 5) sts at beg of foll alt row

and at same time dec 1 st at neck edge of
next and foll alt row.

Work 1 row.

Cast off rem 3 (4: 4: 4: 5: 6) sts.

With RS facing, rejoin yarn to rem sts, cast off
centre 23 (23: 25: 25: 27: 27) sts, P to end.

Complete to match first side, reversing
shapings.

POCKET LININGS (make 2)

Cast on 17 (19: 19: 20: 20: 21) sts using
5mm (US 8) needles.

Beg with a K row, work in st st for 26 (26: 28:
28: 30: 30) rows, ending with a WS row.

Break yarn and leave sts on a holder.

LEFT FRONT

Cast on 45 (47: 49: 51: 53: 56) sts using
4mm (US 6) needles.

Row 1 (RS): P0 (0: 2: 0: 0: 0), K1 (3: 3: 1: 3:
0), *P3, K3, rep from * to last 14 sts, P3, K1,
(P1, K1) 5 times.

Row 2: P1, (K1, P1) 5 times, *K3, P3, rep from
* to last 4 (0: 2: 4: 0: 3) sts, K3 (0: 2: 3: 0: 3),
P1 (0: 0: 1: 0: 0).

Row 3: P0 (0: 2: 0: 0: 0), K1 (3: 3: 1: 3: 0),
*P3, K3, rep from * to last 14 sts, P4, (K1, P1)
5 times.

Row 4: K1, (P1, K1) 5 times, *K3, P3, rep from
* to last 4 (0: 2: 4: 0: 3) sts, K3 (0: 2: 3: 0: 3),
P1 (0: 0: 1: 0: 0).

Row 5: K0 (0: 2: 0: 0: 0), P1 (3: 3: 1: 3: 0),
*K3, P3, rep from * to last 14 sts, K4, (P1, K1)
5 times.

Row 6: P1, (K1, P1) 5 times, *P3, K3, rep from
* to last 4 (0: 2: 4: 0: 3) sts, P3 (0: 2: 3: 0: 3),
K1 (0: 0: 1: 0: 0).

Row 7: K0 (0: 2: 0: 0: 0), P1 (3: 3: 1: 3: 0),
*K3, P3, rep from * to last 14 sts, K3, P1, (K1,
P1) 5 times.

Row 8: K1, (P1, K1) 5 times, *P3, K3, rep from
* to last 4 (0: 2: 4: 0: 3) sts, P3 (0: 2: 3: 0: 3),
K1 (0: 0: 1: 0: 0).

These 8 rows set the sts – front opening edge
11 sts in double moss st with all other sts in
basket st patt.

Cont as set for a further 12 (16: 16: 20: 20:
24) rows, ending with a WS row.

Change to 5mm (US 8) needles.

Next row (RS): P to last 11 sts, patt 11 sts.

Next row: Patt 11 sts, K to end.

These 2 rows set the sts – front opening edge 11 sts still in double moss st with all other sts now in rev st st.

Shorter cardigan only

Cont as set for a further 16 (16: 14: 14: 12: 12) rows, ending with a WS row.

Longer cardigan only

Cont as set for a further 40 (40: 38: 38: 36: 36) rows, ending with a WS row.

Both cardigans

Place pocket

Next row (RS): P8 (8: 9: 10: 11: 13), slip next 17 (19: 19: 20: 20: 21) sts onto a holder and, in their place, P across 17 (19: 19: 20: 20: 21) sts of first pocket lining, patt to end.

Cont straight until 60 rows less have been worked than on back to beg of armhole shaping, ending with a WS row.

Shape front slope

Next row (RS): P to last 13 sts, P2tog, patt to end.

Working all front slope decreases as set by last row, dec 1 st at front slope edge of 10th (10th: 8th: 8th: 8th: 8th) and 0 (0: 2: 2: 6: 6) foll 8th rows, then on 4 (4: 3: 3: 0: 0) foll 10th rows. 39 (41: 42: 44: 45: 48) sts.

Work 9 (9: 5: 5: 3: 3) rows, ending with a WS row.

Shape armhole

Cast off 4 sts at beg and dec 1 (1: 0: 0: 0: 0) st at front slope edge of next row. 34 (36: 38: 40: 41: 44) sts.

Work 1 row.

Dec 1 st at armhole edge of next 5 (5: 7: 7: 7: 9) rows, then on foll 3 (4: 2: 3: 3: 3) alt rows, then on foll 4th row **and at same time** dec 1 st at front slope edge of 9th (9th: 3rd: 3rd: 5th: 5th) and 0 (0: 1: 1: 1: 1) foll 10th row. 24 (25: 26: 27: 28: 29) sts.

Dec 1 st at front slope edge only on 4th (2nd: 8th: 6th: 8th: 6th) and foll 10th row. 22 (23: 24: 25: 26: 27) sts.

Cont straight until left front matches back to beg of shoulder shaping, ending with a WS row.

Shape shoulder

Cast off 4 (4: 5: 5: 5: 5) sts at beg of next row, then 4 (4: 4: 5: 5: 5) sts at beg of foll alt row.

Work 1 row.

Next row (RS): Cast off 3 (4: 4: 4: 5: 6) sts, inc in next st, patt to end.

Cont in double moss st on these 12 sts only (for back neck border extension) for a further 9 (9: 9.5: 9.5: 10: 10) cm, ending with a WS row.

Cast off in patt.

Mark positions for 4 buttons along front opening edge – first to come in row 5, last to come 1.5 cm down from beg of front slope shaping, and rem 2 buttons evenly spaced between.

RIGHT FRONT

Cast on 45 (47: 49: 51: 53: 56) sts using 4mm (US 6) needles.

Row 1 (RS): (K1, P1) 5 times, K1, *P3, K3, rep from * to last 4 (0: 2: 4: 0: 3) sts, P3 (0: 2: 3: 0: 3), K1 (0: 0: 1: 0: 0).

Row 2: K0 (0: 2: 0: 0: 0), P1 (3: 3: 1: 3: 0), *K3, P3, rep from * to last 14 sts, K3, P1, (K1, P1) 5 times.

Row 3: (P1, K1) 5 times, P1, *P3, K3, rep from * to last 4 (0: 2: 4: 0: 3) sts, P3 (0: 2: 3: 0: 3), K1 (0: 0: 1: 0: 0).

Row 4: K0 (0: 2: 0: 0: 0), P1 (3: 3: 1: 3: 0), *K3, P3, rep from * to last 14 sts, K4, (P1, K1) 5 times.

These 4 rows set the sts – front opening edge 11 sts in double moss st with all other sts in basket st patt.

Keeping sts correct as now set, cont as folls:

Row 5 (buttonhole row 1): Patt 4 sts, cast off 3 sts (to make a buttonhole), patt to end.

Row 6 (buttonhole row 2): Patt to cast-off sts, (yrn) 3 times, patt 4 sts.

Row 7 (buttonhole row 3): Patt 4 sts, patt across next 3 yrn's working into back loops, patt to end.

Working a further 3 buttonholes in this way to correspond with positions marked for buttons on left front and noting that no further reference will be made to buttonholes, cont as folls:

Cont as set for a further 13 (17: 17: 21: 21: 25) rows, ending with a WS row.

Change to 5mm (US 8) needles.

Next row (RS): Patt 11 sts, P to end.

Next row: K to last 11 sts, patt 11 sts.

These 2 rows set the sts – front opening edge 11 sts still in double moss st with all other sts now in rev st st.

Shorter cardigan only

Cont as set for a further 16 (16: 14: 14: 12: 12) rows, ending with a WS row.

Longer cardigan only

Cont as set for a further 40 (40: 38: 38: 36: 36) rows, ending with a WS row.

Both cardigans

Place pocket

Next row (RS): Patt 20 (20: 21: 21: 22: 22) sts, slip next 17 (19: 19: 20: 20: 21) sts onto a holder and, in their place, P across 17 (19: 19: 20: 20: 21) sts of second pocket lining, P to end.

Cont straight until 60 rows less have been worked than on back to beg of armhole shaping, ending with a WS row.

Shape front slope

Next row (RS): Patt 11 sts, P2tog, P to end.

Working all front slope decreases as set by last row, complete to match left front, reversing shapings.

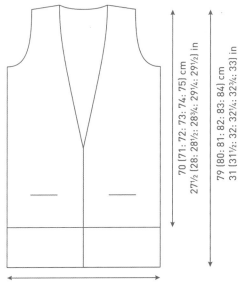

70 (71: 72: 73: 74: 75) cm
27½ (28: 28½: 28¾: 29¼: 29½) in

79 (80: 81: 82: 83: 84) cm
31 (31½: 32: 32¼: 32¾: 33) in

48 (50.5: 53: 55.5: 58: 62) cm
19 (20: 20¾: 22: 22¾: 24½) in

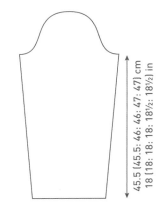

45.5 (45.5: 46: 46: 47: 47) cm
18 (18: 18: 18: 18½: 18½) in

Recommendation
Suitable for the novice knitter
Please see pages 46 & 47 for photographs.

One size

Rowan Calmer
1 x 50gm
Photographed in Cloud

Needles
1 pair 4mm (no 8) (US 6) needles
1 pair 5mm (no 6) (US 8) needles

Tension
21 sts and 30 rows to 10 cm measured over
stocking stitch using 5mm (US 8) needles.

CHEER
Close fitting textured hat

HAT
Cast on 106 sts using 4mm (US 6) needles.
Work in garter st for 20 rows, ending with
a WS row.
Change to 5mm (US 8) needles.
Row 1 (RS): Knit.
Row 2: Purl.
Rows 3 and 4: Knit.
Row 5: Purl.
Rows 6 and 7: Knit.
Row 8: Purl.
Rows 9 and 10: Knit.
Row 11: Purl.
Row 12: Knit.
Rows 13 to 16: As rows 11 and 12, twice.
Rows 17 to 23: As rows 1 to 7.
Row 24 (WS): K1, *yfwd, sl 1, K1, psso, rep from
* to last st, K1.
Row 25: As row 24.
Rows 26 and 27: As rows 1 and 2.
Row 28: K2tog, K to end. 105 sts.
Shape top
Row 1 (RS): *K11, K2tog, rep from * to last st,
K1. 97 sts.
Row 2: Purl.

Rows 3 and 4: Knit.
Row 5: Purl.
Row 6: Knit.
Row 7: *K10, K2tog, rep from * to last st, K1.
89 sts.
Row 8 and every foll alt row: Purl.
Row 9: Knit.
Row 11: *K9, K2tog, rep from * to last st, K1.
81 sts.
Row 13: *K8, K2tog, rep from * to last st, K1.
73 sts.
Row 15: *K7, K2tog, rep from * to last st, K1.
65 sts.
Row 17: *K6, K2tog, rep from * to last st, K1.
57 sts.
Row 19: *K5, K2tog, rep from * to last st, K1.
49 sts.
Row 21: *K3, K3tog, rep from * to last st, K1.
33 sts.
Row 23: *K1, K3tog, rep from * to last st, K1.
17 sts.
Row 24: Purl.
Break yarn and thread through rem 17 sts. Pull
up tight and fasten off securely. Join back seam,
preferably using mattress stitch.

Bud — Continued from previous page.

SLEEVES (both alike)
Cast on 39 (39: 41: 41: 43: 43) sts using
4mm (US 6) needles.
Row 1 (RS): K0 (0: 1: 1: 2: 2), *P3, K3, rep
from * to last 3 (3: 4: 4: 5: 5) sts, P3, K0 (0: 1:
1: 2: 2).
Row 2: P0 (0: 1: 1: 2: 2), *K3, P3, rep from *
to last 3 (3: 4: 4: 5: 5) sts, K3, P0 (0: 1: 1: 2: 2).
Rows 3 and 4: As rows 1 and 2.
Row 5: As row 2.
Row 6: As row 1.
Rows 7 and 8: As rows 5 and 6.
These 8 rows form basket st patt.
Work in basket st patt for a further 16 rows,
ending with a WS row.
Change to 5mm (US 8) needles.
Beg with a P row, now work in rev st st,

shaping sides by inc 1 st at each end of 5th
and every foll 10th row to 49 (49: 51: 51: 53:
53) sts, then on every foll 12th row until there
are 53 (53: 55: 55: 57: 57) sts.
Cont straight until sleeve measures 45.5 (45.5:
46: 46: 47: 47) cm, ending with a WS row.
Shape top
Cast off 4 sts at beg of next 2 rows.
45 (45: 47: 47: 49: 49) sts.
Dec 1 st at each end of next 3 rows, then
on foll alt row, then on 4 (4: 5: 5: 5: 5) foll
4th rows. 29 (29: 29: 29: 31: 31) sts.
Work 1 row.
Dec 1 st at each end of next and foll 1 (1: 1:
1: 2: 2) alt rows, then on foll 5 (5: 3: 3: 3: 3)
rows, ending with a WS row.
Cast off rem 15 (15: 19: 19: 19: 19) sts.

MAKING UP
Pin the pieces out and steam gently without
allowing the iron to touch the yarn.
Join both shoulder seams using back stitch or
mattress stitch if preferred. Join cast-off edges
of back neck border extensions, then sew one
edge to back neck.
Pocket tops (both alike)
Slip 17 (19: 19: 20: 20: 21) sts from pocket
holder onto 4mm (US 6) needles and rejoin
yarn with RS facing.
Beg with a P row, work in rev st st for 3 rows,
ending with a **RS** row. Cast off knitwise (on **WS**).
Sew pocket linings in place on inside, allowing
pocket tops to roll to inside.
Join side seams. Join sleeve seams. Insert
sleeves into armholes. Sew on buttons.

BLOSSOM

Sculptured peplum cardigan with nipped in waist

Recommendation

Suitable for the knitter with a little experience
Please see pages 16 & 17 for photographs.

	XS	S	M	L	XL	XXL	
To fit bust	**81**	**86**	**91**	**97**	**102**	**109**	cm
	32	34	36	38	40	43	in

Rowan Fine Milk Cotton

	5	6	6	7	7	8	x 50gm

Photographed in Navy

Needles

1 pair 2¼mm (no 13) (US 1) needles
1 pair 2¾mm (no 12) (US 2) needles

Buttons – 3

Tension

26 sts and 42 rows to 10 cm measured over
main pattern using 2¾mm (US 2) needles.

SPECIAL ABBREVIATION

MP = make picot as folls: cast on 1 st, then
cast off 1 st.

BACK

Lower edging

Cast on 28 (28: 28: 30: 30: 30) sts using
2¾mm (US 2) needles.
Row 1 (RS): K to last 5 sts, yfwd, K2tog, K3.
Row 2: sl 1, K4, yfwd, K2tog, K3, wrap next
st (by slipping next st on left needle onto
right needle, taking yarn to opposite side of
work between needles and then slipping same
st back onto left needle – when working back
across wrapped sts work the wrapped st and
the wrapping loop tog as one st) and turn.
Row 3: K5, yfwd, K2tog, K3.
Row 4: sl 1, K4, yfwd, K2tog, K11, wrap next
st and turn.
Row 5: K13, yfwd, K2tog, K3.
Row 6: sl 1, K4, yfwd, K2tog, K19, wrap next
st and turn.
Row 7: K21, yfwd, K2tog, inc once in each
of next 3 sts.
31 (31: 31: 33: 33: 33) sts.
Row 8: Cast off 3 sts, K until there are 5 sts
on right needle, yfwd, K2tog, K to end.
28 (28: 28: 30: 30: 30) sts.
These 8 rows complete side seam shaping.
Now work in edging patt as folls:
Row 1 (RS): K to last 5 sts, yfwd, K2tog, K3.
Row 2: sl 1, K4, yfwd, K2tog, K to end.
Rows 3 and 4: As rows 1 and 2.
Row 5: K to last 5 sts, yfwd, K2tog, inc once
in each of next 3 sts.
Row 6: Cast off 3 sts, K until there are 5 sts
on right needle, yfwd, K2tog, K to end.
These 6 rows form edging patt.**
Rep last 6 rows 30 (32: 35: 37: 40: 43) times
more, ending with a WS row.
***Now shape second side seam as folls:
Row 1 (RS): K to last 5 sts, yfwd, K2tog, K3.
Row 2: sl 1, K4, yfwd, K2tog, K19, wrap next
st and turn.
Row 3: K21, yfwd, K2tog, K3.
Row 4: sl 1, K4, yfwd, K2tog, K11, wrap next
st and turn.
Row 5: K13, yfwd, K2tog, K3.
Row 6: sl 1, K4, yfwd, K2tog, K3, wrap next
st and turn.

Row 7: K5, yfwd, K2tog, K3.
Row 8: sl 1, K4, yfwd, K2tog, K to end.
Cast off.***
Upper back
With RS facing and using 2¾mm (US 2)
needles, pick up and knit 86 (92: 98: 104:
112: 124) sts evenly along straight row-end
edge of lower edging.
Next row (WS): Purl.
Now work in main patt as folls:
Row 1 (RS): Knit.
Row 2: Purl.
Rows 3 to 6: As rows 1 and 2, twice.
Row 7: K1, *yfwd, sl 1, K1, psso, rep from * to
last st, K1.
Rows 8 and 9: As row 7.
Row 10: Purl.
Row 11: Inc twice in first st, K to last st, inc
twice in last st.
90 (96: 102: 108: 116: 128) sts.
Row 12: Purl.
Rows 13 and 14: As rows 1 and 2.
Row 15: Knit.
Rows 16 to 18: As row 7.
These 18 rows form main patt and beg side
seam shaping.
Cont in patt, inc 2 sts (as set by row 11) at
each end of 11th and 3 foll 18th rows, taking
inc sts into patt.
106 (112: 118: 124: 132: 144) sts.
Work 7 (7: 11: 11: 11: 11) rows, ending with
a WS row. (Back should measure 22 (22: 23:
23: 23: 23) cm from pick-up row.)
Shape armholes
Keeping patt correct, cast off 6 (6: 6: 7: 7: 7)
sts at beg of next 2 rows.
94 (100: 106: 110: 118: 130) sts.
Dec 1 st at each end of next 5 (5: 7: 7: 9: 11)
rows, then on foll 3 (3: 2: 2: 2: 4) alt rows,
then on foll 4th row.
76 (82: 86: 90: 94: 98) sts.
Cont straight until armhole measures 17 (18:
18: 19: 20: 21) cm, ending with a WS row.
Shape back neck and shoulders
Next row (RS): Patt 21 (23: 24: 25: 26: 27)
sts and turn, leaving rem sts on a holder.

Work each side of neck separately.

Keeping patt correct, dec 1 st at beg of next row, then cast off 6 (7: 7: 8: 8: 8) sts at beg of foll row.

Rep last 2 rows once more.

Work 1 row.

Cast off rem 7 (7: 8: 7: 8: 9) sts.

With RS facing, rejoin yarn to rem sts, cast off centre 34 (36: 38: 40: 42: 44) sts, patt to end.

Complete to match first side, reversing shapings.

LEFT FRONT
Lower edging

Work as given for lower edging of back to **.

Place marker at beg of last row.

Rep last 6 rows 10 (11: 12: 13: 14: 16) times more, then rows 1 to 4 again, ending with a WS row.

Now shape front curve as folls:

Row 1 (RS): K to last 8 sts, K2tog, K1, yfwd, K2tog, inc once in each of next 3 sts.

Work 3 rows. 27 (27: 27: 29: 29: 29) sts.

Row 5: K to last 8 sts, K2tog, K1, yfwd, K2tog, K3.

26 (26: 26: 28: 28: 28) sts.

Work 3 rows.

Row 9: As row 5. 25 (25: 25: 27: 27: 27) sts.

Work 3 rows.

Rep rows 1 to 5 (5: 5: 9: 9: 9) once more.

23 (23: 23: 24: 24: 24) sts.

Work 1 row, ending with a WS row.

Keeping patt correct, dec 1 st as now set on next and every foll alt row until 9 sts rem.

Next row (WS): Patt to last 2 sts, K2tog. 8 sts.

Keeping patt correct as much as possible and then working all sts in g st, dec 1 st at beg of next row and at same edge on foll 6 rows. 1 st.

Fasten off.

Upper left front

With RS facing and using 2¾mm (US 2) needles, pick up and knit 54 (57: 60: 63: 67: 73) sts evenly along straight row-end edge of lower edging, between cast-on edge and fasten-off point.

Next row (WS): Purl.

Now work in patt as folls:

Row 1 (RS): Knit.

Row 2: MP, K until there are 12 sts on right needle, P to end.

Row 3: Knit.

Row 4: K12, P to end.

Rows 5 and 6: As rows 1 and 2.

Row 7: K1, *yfwd, sl 1, K1, psso, rep from * to last 13 (12: 13: 12: 12: 12) sts, K13 (12: 13: 12: 12: 12).

Row 8: K13 (12: 13: 12: 12: 12), *yfwd, sl 1, K1, psso, rep from * to last st, K1.

Row 9: As row 7.

Row 10: As row 2.

Row 11: Inc twice in first st, K to end.

56 (59: 62: 65: 69: 75) sts.

Row 12: As row 4.

Rows 13 and 14: As rows 1 and 2.

Row 15: Knit.

Row 16: As row 8.

Row 17: As row 7.

Row 18: As row 8.

These 18 rows set the sts - main patt with front opening edge 12 sts worked in g st with picot worked at front opening edge on every alt WS row - and beg side seam shaping.

Cont as set for 10 rows, ending with a WS row.

Shape front slope

Next row (RS): Inc twice in first st, patt to last 14 sts, K2tog, K12.

57 (60: 63: 66: 70: 76) sts.

Working all front slope decreases as set by last row, dec 1 st at front slope edge of 6th and 6 (8: 9: 9: 9: 9) foll 6th rows, then on 2 (0: 0: 0: 0: 0) foll 8th rows **and at same time** inc 2 sts at beg of 18th and 2 foll 18th rows, taking inc sts into patt.

54 (57: 59: 62: 66: 72) sts.

Work 3 (7: 5: 5: 5: 5) rows, ending with a WS row.

Shape armhole

Keeping patt correct, cast off 6 (6: 6: 7: 7: 7) sts at beg and dec 0 (1: 1: 1: 1: 1) st at front slope edge of next row.

48 (50: 52: 54: 58: 64) sts.

Work 1 row.

Dec 1 st at armhole edge of next 5 (5: 7: 7: 9: 11) rows, then on foll 3 (3: 2: 2: 2: 4) alt rows, then on foll 4th row **and at same time** dec 1 st at front slope edge of 3rd (7th: 7th: 5th: 5th: 5th) and 1 (1: 1: 1: 2: 3) foll 8th (8th: 8th: 6th: 6th: 6th) rows.

37 (39: 40: 42: 43: 44) sts.

Dec 1 st at front slope edge **only** on 4th (8th: 8th: 4th: 6th: 6th) and 0 (0: 0: 0: 0: 1) foll 6th row, then on 5 (5: 5: 6: 6: 5) foll 8th rows.

31 (33: 34: 35: 36: 37) sts.

Cont straight until left front matches back to beg of shoulder shaping, ending with a WS row.

Shape shoulder

Keeping patt correct, cast off 6 (7: 7: 8: 8: 8) sts at beg of next and foll alt row, then 7 (7: 8: 7: 8: 9) sts at beg of foll alt row. 12 sts.

Inc 1 st at end of next row. 13 sts.

Cont in patt on these 13 sts only for a further 8.5 (9: 9.5: 10: 10.5: 11) cm for back neck border extension, ending with a WS row.

Cast off.

RIGHT FRONT
Lower edging

Cast on 1 st using 2¾mm (US 2) needles.

Row 1 (RS): Inc in st. 2 sts.

Row 2: K1, inc in last st. 3 sts.

Row 3: Inc in first st, K2. 4 sts.

Row 4: K3, inc in last st. 5 sts.

Row 5: Inc in first st, K4. 6 sts.

Row 6: K5, inc in last st. 7 sts.

Row 7: Inc in first st, K1, yfwd, K2tog, K3. 8 sts.

Row 8: K5, inc in next st, K2. 9 sts.

Row 9: K2, inc in next st, K1, yfwd, K2tog, inc once in each of last 3 sts.

Row 10: Cast off 3 sts, K until there are 5 sts on right needle, inc in next st, K4. 11 sts.

Row 11: K to last 7 sts, inc in next st, K1, yfwd, K2tog, K3. 12 sts.

Row 12: K5, yfwd, K2tog, K to end.

These 12 rows set patt and beg front curve shaping.

Keeping patt correct, inc 1 st (as set by row 11) on next and every foll alt row to 24 (24: 24: 25: 25: 25) sts, then on every foll 4th row until there are 28 (28: 28: 30: 30: 30) sts.

Cont straight until straight row-end edge of this edging measures same as straight row-end edge of lower left front edging from fasten-off point to marker, ending with a WS row.

Now work as given for lower edging of back from *** to ***.

Upper right front

With RS facing and using 2¾mm (US 2) needles, pick up and knit 54 (57: 60: 63: 67: 73) sts evenly along straight row-end edge of lower edging, between fasten-off point and cast-off edge.

Next row (WS): Purl.

Now work in patt as folls:

Row 1 (RS): MP, K until there are 5 sts on right needle, K2tog, yfwd (to make first buttonhole), K to end.

Row 2: P to last 12 sts, K12.

Row 3: Knit.

Row 4: As row 2.

Row 5: MP, K to end.

Row 6: As row 2.

Row 7: K13 (12: 13: 12: 12: 12), *yfwd, sl 1, K1, psso, rep from * to last st, K1.

Row 8: K1, *yfwd, sl 1, K1, psso, rep from * to last 13 (12: 13: 12: 12: 12) sts, K13 (12: 13: 12: 12: 12).

Row 9: MP, K until there are 13 (12: 13: 12: 12: 12) sts on right needle, *yfwd, sl 1, K1, psso, rep from * to last st, K1.

Row 10: As row 2.

Row 11: K5, K2tog, yfwd (to make second buttonhole), K to last st, inc twice in last st. 56 (59: 62: 65: 69: 75) sts.

Row 12: As row 2.

Row 13: As row 5.

Row 14: As row 2.

Row 15: Knit.

Row 16: As row 8.

Row 17: As row 9.

Row 18: As row 8.

These 18 rows set the sts - main patt with front opening edge 12 sts worked in g st with picot worked at front opening edge on every alt RS row - and beg side seam shaping.

Cont as set for 2 rows, ending with a WS row.

Row 21 (RS): Patt 5 sts, K2tog, yfwd (to make 3rd buttonhole), patt to end.

Cont as set for a further 7 rows, ending with a WS row.

Shape front slope

Next row (RS): Patt 12 sts, K2tog tbl, patt to last st, inc twice in last st. 57 (60: 63: 66: 70: 76) sts.

Working all front slope decreases as set by last row, complete to match left front, reversing shapings.

SLEEVES (both alike)
Edging

Cast on 6 sts using 2¼mm (US 1) needles.

Row 1 (RS): MP, K to end.

Row 2: Knit.

Rep these 2 rows until 136 (142: 148: 154: 160: 166) rows in total have been worked, ending with a WS row.

Cast off but do NOT break yarn.

Upper sleeve

With RS facing and using 2¾mm (US 2) needles, pick up and knit 84 (88: 92: 94: 98: 102) sts evenly along straight row-end edge of edging.

Beg with a P row, work in st st for 3 (3: 3: 5: 5: 5) rows, ending with a WS row.

Shape top
Sizes XS, S and M

Row 1 (RS): Cast off 6 (8: 8: -: -: -) sts, K to end.

Row 2: Cast off 6 (8: 8: -: -: -) sts, P to end. 72 (72: 76: -: -: -) sts.

Row 3: Cast off 3 sts (one st on right needle), *yfwd, sl 1, K1, psso, rep from * to end.

Row 4: Cast off 3 sts (one st on right needle), *yfwd, sl 1, K1, psso, rep from * to last st, K1. 66 (66: 70: -: -: -) sts.

These 4 rows set position of main patt and beg sleeve top shaping.

Sizes L, XL and XXL

Row 1 (RS): Cast off – (-: -: 9: 9: 11) sts (one st on right needle), *yfwd, sl 1, K1, psso, rep from * to end.

Row 2: Cast off – (-: -: 9: 9: 11) sts (one st on right needle), *yfwd, sl 1, K1, psso, rep from * to last st, K1. - (-: -: 76: 80: 80) sts.

These 2 rows set position of main patt and beg sleeve top shaping.

All sizes

Keeping patt correct as now set, cast off 3 sts at beg of next 2 (2: 2: 4: 4: 4) rows. 60 (60: 64: 64: 68: 68) sts.

Dec 1 st at each end of next 16 (16: 18: 18: 20: 20) rows, ending with a WS row. 28 sts.

Cast off 3 sts at beg of next 4 rows.

Cast off rem 16 sts.

MAKING UP

Press all pieces using a warm iron over a damp cloth.

Join both shoulder seams using back stitch or mattress stitch if preferred. Join cast-off ends of back neck border extensions, then neatly sew one edge to back neck edge.

Join side seams. Join sleeve seams.

Set sleeves into armholes. Sew on buttons.

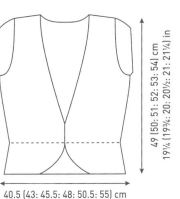

49 (50: 51: 52: 53: 54) cm
19¼ (19¾: 20: 20½: 21: 21¼) in

40.5 (43: 45.5: 48: 50.5: 55) cm
16 (17: 18: 19: 20: 21¾) in

LILY

Close-fitting shrug with single button & garter stitch trim

Recommendation

Suitable for the knitter with a little experience
Please see page 19 for photograph.

	XS	S	M	L	XL	XXL	
To fit bust	**81**	**86**	**91**	**97**	**102**	**107**	cm
	32	34	36	38	40	42	in

Rowan Summer Tweed

| | 6 | 7 | 7 | 7 | 8 | 8 x 50gm |

Photographed in Storm

Needles

1 pair 4½ mm (no 7) (US 7) needles
1 pair 5 mm (no 6) (US 8) needles

Button – 1

Tension

16 sts and 23 rows to 10cm measured over
stocking stitch using 5 mm (US 8) needles.

Special abbreviations

MP = Make picot: cast on 1 st, cast off 1 st.
Right dec = Slip 1, K1, psso, slip st now on
right needle back onto left needle, lift 2nd st
on left needle over this st and off left needle,
and then slip rem st back onto right needle –
2 sts decreased.
Left dec = Slip 1, K2tog, psso – 2 sts
decreased.

BACK

Lower edging (knitted from side to side)
Cast on 11 (12: 12: 12: 13: 13) sts using 4½
mm (US 7) needles.
Row 1 (RS): MP, K to end.
Row 2: Knit.
Rep these 2 rows until 120 (128: 136: 144:
152: 164) rows in all completed, ending with
a WS row.
Cast off, but do not break the yarn.

Upper back
With RS of lower edging facing and using
5 mm (US 8) needles, pick up and knit
60 (64: 68: 72: 76: 82) sts evenly along the
top (straight) edge of edging, then purl 1 row,
ending with a WS row.
Beg with a K row, cont in st st as folls:
Work 4 rows.
Next row (RS) (inc): K3, M1, K to last 3 sts,
M1, K3. 62 (66: 70: 74: 78: 84) sts.
Work 7 rows, ending with a WS row.
Inc 1 st as before at each end of next row.
64 (68: 72: 76: 80: 86) sts.
Work 7 (7: 9: 9: 9: 11) rows, ending with
a WS row.
Shape armholes
Cast off 4 (4: 4: 4: 4: 5) sts at beg of next
2 rows. 56 (60: 64: 68: 72: 76) sts.
Dec 1 st at each end of next 3 rows and
0 (1: 2: 3: 3: 4) foll alt rows.
50 (52: 54: 56: 60: 62) sts.
Cont straight until armhole measures 18 (19:
19: 20: 21: 22) cm, ending with a WS row.
Shape shoulders and back neck
Cast off 5 sts at beg of next 2 rows.
40 (42: 44: 46: 50: 52) sts.
Next row (RS): Cast off 5 sts, K until there are
7 (8: 9: 8: 10: 11) sts on right needle and turn
leaving rem sts on a holder.
Work each side of neck separately.
Next row: Cast off 4 sts, P to end.
Cast off rem 3 (4: 5: 4: 6: 7) sts.
With RS facing rejoin yarn to rem sts, cast off
centre 16 (16: 16: 20: 20: 20) sts, K to end.
Complete to match first side reversing
shapings.

LEFT FRONT

Cast on 17 (19: 21: 23: 25: 28) sts using
5 mm (US 8) needles and shape front edge
as folls:
Row 1 (RS) (inc): Knit 1 row, turn and cast
on 3 sts. 20 (22: 24: 26: 28: 31) sts.
Row 2: Purl.
Inc 1 st at front edge on next 4 rows.
24 (26: 28: 30: 32: 35) sts.
Next row (RS) (inc): K3, M1, K to end, inc 1 st
at end of row. 26 (28: 30: 32: 34: 37) sts.
Work 1 row.
Inc 1 st at front edge of next row and 2 foll alt
rows, ending with a RS row.
29 (31: 33: 35: 37: 40) sts.
Work 1 row.
Next row (RS) (inc): K3, M1, K to end, inc 1 st
at end of row. 31 (33: 35: 37: 39: 42) sts.
Work 1 row.
Inc 1 st at front edge of next row.
32 (34: 36: 38: 40: 43) sts.
Work straight for 5 (5: 7: 7: 7: 9) rows, ending
with a WS row.
Shape armhole and front neck
Cast off 4 (4: 4: 4: 4: 5) sts at beg of next row.
28 (30: 32: 34: 36: 38) sts.
Work 1 row.
Next row (RS) (dec): K2tog, K to last 5 sts,
left dec, K2.
Dec 1 st at armhole edge as given for back on
the next 2 rows and follow 0 (1: 2: 3: 3: 4) foll
alt rows, and **at the same time** dec 2 sts at
front edge as before on 3 foll 6th rows, ending
with a RS row.
17 (18: 19: 20: 22: 23) sts.
Work 7 rows.
Dec 2 sts as before at front edge on next row
and 1 (1: 1: 2: 2: 2) foll 8th rows.
13 (14: 15: 14: 16: 17) sts.
Cont straight until front matches back to beg
of shoulder shaping, ending with a WS row.
Shape shoulder
Cast off 5 sts at beg of next row and foll alt row.
Work 1 row.
Cast off rem 3 (4: 5: 4: 6: 7) sts.

RIGHT FRONT

Cast on 17 (19: 21: 23: 25: 28) sts using
5 mm (US 8) needles and shape front edge
as folls:

Row 1 (RS): Knit.

Row 2 (inc): Purl to end, turn and cast
on 4 sts.

21 (23: 25: 27: 29: 32) sts.

Row 3: Knit.

Inc 1 st at front edge on the next 3 rows.

24 (26: 28: 30: 32: 35) sts.

Next row (RS) (inc): Inc in first stitch, K to
last 3 sts, M1, K3.

26 (28: 30: 32: 34: 37) sts.

Work 1 row.

Inc 1 st at front edge of next row and 2 foll alt
rows, ending with a RS row.

29 (31: 33: 35: 37: 40) sts.

Work 1 row.

Next row (RS) (inc): Inc in first stitch, K to
last 3 sts, M1, K3.

31 (33: 35: 37: 39: 42) sts.

Work 1 row.

Inc 1 st at front edge of next row.

32 (34: 36: 38: 40: 43) sts.

Work straight for 6 (6: 8: 8: 8: 10) rows,
ending with a **RS** row.

Shape armhole and front neck

Cast off 4 (4: 4: 4: 4: 5) sts at beg of
next row.

28 (30: 32: 34: 36: 38) sts.

Next row (RS) (dec): K2, right dec, K to last
2 sts, K2tog.

Dec 1 st at armhole edge as given for back on
the next 2 rows and follow 0 (1: 2: 3: 3: 4) foll
alt rows, and **at the same time** dec 2 sts at
front edge as before on 3 foll 6th rows, ending
with a RS row.

17 (18: 19: 20: 22: 23) sts.

Complete to match first side, reversing
shapings.

SLEEVES (both alike)

Lower edging (knitted from side to side)

Cast on 11 (12: 12: 12: 13: 13) sts using
4½ mm (US 7) needles.

Knit 2 rows.

Next row (RS): MP, K to end.

Knit 1 row.

Working a picot at beg of every RS row, cont in
garter st for a further 82 (86: 90: 94: 98: 102)
rows, ending with a WS row.

Cast off, but do not break yarn.

Upper sleeve

With RS of lower edging facing and using
5 mm (US 8) needles, pick up and knit 44
(46: 48: 48: 50: 52) sts evenly along the top
(straight) edge of edging, then purl 1 row,
ending with a WS row.

Beg with a K row, cont in st st as folls:

Work 14 rows.

Next row (RS) (inc): K3, M1, K to last 3 sts,
M1, K3.

46 (48: 50: 50: 52: 54) sts.

Work 15 rows, ending with a WS row.

Inc as before at each end of next row and foll
16th row.

50 (52: 54: 54: 56: 58) sts.

Cont straight until sleeve measures
31 (32: 33: 34: 35: 36) cm, ending
with a WS row.

Shape sleeve top

Cast off 4 sts at beg of next 2 rows.

42 (44: 46: 46: 48: 50) sts.

Dec 1 st at each end of next 3 rows.

36 (38: 40: 40: 42: 44) sts.

Work 3 rows.

Dec 1 st at each end of next row and then
on 4 (3: 4: 4: 4: 4) foll 4th rows and 2 (4: 1:
3: 3: 4) foll alt rows, and then on every row
to 16 (16: 18: 18: 20: 20) sts.

Cast off.

MAKING UP

Press all pieces using a warm iron.

Join both shoulder seams using back stitch or
mattress stitch if preferred.

Join side and sleeve seams.

Set sleeves into armholes.

Place a marker for the buttonhole on the
right front, immediately after lower front edge
shaping is completed.

Front edging

Cast on 11 (12: 12: 12: 13: 13) sts using
4½ mm (US 7) needles.

Row 1 (RS): MP, K to end.

Row 2: Knit.

Cont in garter st working a picot at the
beg of every RS row until edging fits neatly
and not stretched from right side seam to
buttonhole marker on right front, ending
with a WS row.

Buttonhole row (RS): K5, cast off 3, K to end.

Next row: Work across row, casting-on 3 sts
over those cast-off on previous row.

11 (12: 12: 12: 13: 13) sts.

Cont in garter stitch until band fits up right
front to shoulder, across back neck, and down
and around left front to left side seam.

Slip stitch neatly into place, adjusting length if
necessary.

Cast off.

Join ends of front and back edgings neatly
together at side seams.

Sew on button.

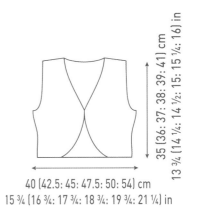

35 (36: 37: 38: 39: 41) cm
13 ¾ (14 ¼: 14 ½: 15: 15 ¼: 16) in

40 (42.5: 45: 47.5: 50: 54) cm
15 ¾ (16 ¾: 17 ¾: 18 ¾: 19 ¾: 21 ¼) in

31 (32: 33: 34: 35: 36) cm
12 ¼ (12 ½: 13: 13 ½: 13 ¾: 14 ¼) in

CARRIE

Textured cardigan with cording & garter stitch trim

Recommendation

Suitable for the knitter with a little experience
Please see page 18 for photograph.

	XS	S	M	L	XL	XXL	
To fit bust	81	86	91	97	102	109	cm
	32	34	36	38	40	43	in

Rowan Fine Milk Cotton

	8	9	9	10	10	11 x 50gm

Photographed in Ardour

Needles

1 pair 2 ¼ m (no 13) (US 1) needles
1 pair 2 ¾ mm (no 12) (US 2) needles
2 double-pointed 2 ¼ mm (no 13) (US 1)
needles

Buttons – 6

Tension

29 sts and 38 rows to 10 cm measured over
main textured pattern using 2 ¾ mm (US 2)
needles.

SPECIAL ABBREVIATIONS

MP = make picot as folls: cast on 1 st, then
cast off 1 st; **dec 2** = slip next 2 sts as though
to K2tog, K1, then pass 2 slipped sts over;
cluster 2 = yrn, P2, lift the yrn over these 2 sts
and off right needle.

Pattern note: When working the lower cluster
patt, the extra sts created within the patt are
NOT included in any stitch counts given.

BACK

Cast on 123 (129: 137: 143: 151: 163) sts
using 2 ¼ mm (US 1) needles.
Work in g st for 16 (16: 18: 18: 20: 20) rows,
ending with a WS row.
Change to 2 ¾ mm (US 2) needles.
Beg with a P row, work in rev st st for 2 rows,
ending with a WS row.
Now work in lower cluster patt as folls:
Row 1 (RS): P7 (4: 2: 5: 3: 3), yon, K1, yfrn,
*P5, yon, K1, yfrn, rep from * to last 7 (4: 2: 5:
3: 3) sts, P7 (4: 2: 5: 3: 3).
Row 2: K7 (4: 2: 5: 3: 3), P3, *K5, P3, rep from
* to last 7 (4: 2: 5: 3: 3) sts, K7 (4: 2: 5: 3: 3).
Row 3: P7 (4: 2: 5: 3: 3), K3, *P5, K3, rep
from * to last 7 (4: 2: 5: 3: 3) sts, P7 (4: 2: 5:
3: 3).
Row 4: As row 2.
Row 5: P2tog, P5 (2: 0: 3: 1: 1), dec 2, *P5,
dec 2, rep from * to last 7 (4: 2: 5: 3: 3) sts,
P5 (2: 0: 3: 1: 1), P2tog.
121 (127: 135: 141: 149: 161) sts.
Row 6: K6 (3: 1: 4: 2: 2), P1, *K5, P1, rep
from * to last 6 (3: 1: 4: 2: 2) sts, K6 (3: 1:
4: 2: 2).
Row 7: P3 (6: 4: 7: 5: 5), yon, K1, yfrn, *P5,
yon, K1, yfrn, rep from * to last 3 (6: 4: 7: 5: 5)
sts, P3 (6: 4: 7: 5: 5).
Row 8: K3 (6: 4: 7: 5: 5), P3, *K5, P3, rep from
* to last 3 (6: 4: 7: 5: 5) sts, K3 (6: 4: 7: 5: 5).
Row 9: P3 (6: 4: 7: 5: 5), K3, *P5, K3, rep
from * to last 3 (6: 4: 7: 5: 5) sts, P3 (6: 4: 7:
5: 5).
Row 10: As row 8.
Row 11: P3 (6: 4: 7: 5: 5), dec 2, *P5, dec 2,
rep from * to last 3 (6: 4: 7: 5: 5) sts, P3 (6: 4:
7: 5: 5).
Row 12: K3 (6: 4: 7: 5: 5), P1, *K5, P1, rep
from * to last 3 (6: 4: 7: 5: 5) sts, K3 (6: 4: 7:
5: 5).
These 12 rows form patt and start side seam
shaping.
Keeping patt correct, work a further 16 rows,
dec 1 st at each end of 5th of these rows and
ending with a WS row.
119 (125: 133: 139: 147: 159) sts.

Next row (dec) (RS): P2tog, patt 17 (20: 18:
21: 19: 25) sts, (P2tog) twice, K1, (P2tog)
twice, patt 63 (63: 75: 75: 87: 87) sts, (P2tog
tbl) twice, K1, (P2tog tbl) twice, patt to last 2
sts, P2tog tbl.
109 (115: 123: 129: 137: 149) sts.
Work 1 row, ending with a WS row.
Beg with a P row, work in rev st st for 2 rows,
ending with a WS row.
Now work in g st for 7 rows, ending with
a **RS** row.
Next row (eyelet row) (WS): P1 (4: 1: 4:
1: 7), (P2tog tbl, yrn, P5) 8 (8: 9: 9: 10: 10)
times, (yrn, P2tog, P5) 7 (7: 8: 8: 9: 9) times,
yrn, P2tog, P1 (4: 1: 4: 1: 7).
Work in g st for 6 rows, dec 1 st at centre
of last row and ending with a WS row.
108 (114: 122: 128: 136: 148) sts.
Now work in main textured patt as folls:
Row 1 (RS): Knit.
Row 2: Purl.
Row 3: Knit.
Row 4: P5 (2: 6: 3: 1: 1), cluster 2, *P4,
cluster 2, rep from * to last 5 (2: 6: 3: 1: 1) sts,
P5 (2: 6: 3: 1: 1).
Rows 5 to 8: As rows 1 and 2, twice.
Row 9: Knit.
Row 10: P2 (5: 3: 6: 4: 4), cluster 2, *P4,
cluster 2, rep from * to last 2 (5: 3: 6: 4: 4) sts,
P2 (5: 3: 6: 4: 4).
Row 11: Inc in first st, K to last st, inc in last
st. 110 (116: 124: 130: 138: 150) sts.
Row 12: Purl.
These 12 rows set position of main textured
patt and beg side seam shaping.
Cont in patt, inc 1 st at each end of 9th
and 2 foll 10th rows, then on 3 foll 8th rows,
taking inc sts into patt.
122 (128: 136: 142: 150: 162) sts.
Cont straight until back measures
35 (35: 36: 36: 37: 37) cm, ending
with a WS row.
Shape armholes
Keeping patt correct, cast off 5 (6: 6: 7: 7: 9)
sts at beg of next 2 rows.
112 (116: 124: 128: 136: 144) sts.

Dec 1 st at each end of next 5 (5: 7: 7: 9: 11) rows, then on foll 4 (4: 4: 4: 4: 5) alt rows, then on foll 4th row.
92 (96: 100: 104: 108: 110) sts.
Cont straight until armhole measures 18 (19: 19: 20: 20: 21) cm, ending with a WS row.
Shape shoulders and back neck
Cast off 9 (9: 9: 10: 10: 10) sts at beg of next 2 rows.
74 (78: 82: 84: 88: 90) sts.
Next row (RS): Cast off 9 (9: 9: 10: 10: 10) sts, patt until there are 12 (13: 14: 13: 14: 14) sts on right needle and turn, leaving rem sts on a holder.
Work each side of neck separately.
Cast off 4 sts at beg of next row.
Cast off rem 8 (9: 10: 9: 10: 10) sts.
With RS facing, rejoin yarn to rem sts, cast off centre 32 (34: 36: 38: 40: 42) sts, patt to end.
Complete to match first side, reversing shapings.

LEFT FRONT
Cast on 71 (74: 78: 81: 85: 91) sts using 2 ¼ mm (US 1) needles.
Row 1 (RS): Knit.
Row 2: MP, K to end.
Rep last 2 rows 7 (7: 8: 8: 9: 9) times more, ending with a WS row.
Change to 2 ¾ mm (US 2) needles.
Next row (RS): P to last 10 sts, K10.
Next row: MP, K to end.
Now work in lower cluster patt as folls:
Row 1 (RS): P7 (4: 2: 5: 3: 3), yon, K1, yfrn, *P5, yon, K1, yfrn, rep from * to last 15 sts, P5, K10.
Row 2: MP, K until there are 15 sts on right needle, P3, *K5, P3, rep from * to last 7 (4: 2: 5: 3: 3) sts, K7 (4: 2: 5: 3: 3).
These 2 rows set the sts – front opening edge 10 sts in g st with picot worked at beg of every WS row and rem sts in lower cluster patt as given for back.
Cont as set, dec 1 st at beg of 3rd and foll 12th row.
69 (72: 76: 79: 83: 89) sts.
Work 11 rows, ending with a WS row.
Next row (dec) (RS): P2tog, patt 17 (20: 18: 21: 19: 25) sts, (P2tog) twice, K1, (P2tog) twice, patt to end.
64 (67: 71: 74: 78: 84) sts.
Work 1 row, ending with a WS row.
Next row (RS): P to last 10 sts, K10.

Next row: MP, K to end.
Working picot at beg of every WS row, now work in g st for 7 rows, ending with a **RS** row.
Next row (eyelet row) (WS): MP, K until there are 10 sts on right needle, P2, (yrn, P2tog, P5) 7 (7: 8: 8: 9: 9) times, yrn, P2tog, P1 (4: 1: 4: 1: 7).
Work in g st with picot edging for a further 6 rows, dec 1 st at centre of last row and ending with a WS row.
63 (66: 70: 73: 77: 83) sts.
Now work in main textured patt as folls:
Row 1 (RS): Knit.
Row 2: MP, K until there are 10 sts on right needle, P to end.
Row 3: Knit.
Row 4: MP, K until there are 10 sts on right needle, *P4, cluster 2, rep from * to last 5 (2: 6: 3: 1: 1) sts, P5 (2: 6: 3: 1: 1).
These 4 rows set the sts - front opening edge 10 sts still in g st with picot worked at beg of every WS row and rem sts now in main textured patt as given for back.
Cont as set, inc 1 st at beg of 7th and 3 foll 10th rows, then on 3 foll 8th rows, taking inc sts into patt. 70 (73: 77: 80: 84: 90) sts.
Cont straight until left front matches back to beg of armhole shaping, ending with a WS row.
Shape armhole
Keeping patt correct, cast off 5 (6: 6: 7: 7: 9) sts at beg of next 2 rows.
65 (67: 71: 73: 77: 81) sts.
Work 1 row.
Dec 1 st at armhole edge of next 5 (5: 7: 7: 9: 11) rows, then on foll 4 (4: 4: 4: 4: 5) alt rows, then on foll 4th row.
55 (57: 59: 61: 63: 64) sts.
Cont straight until 21 (21: 23: 23: 25: 25) rows less have been worked than on back to start of shoulder shaping, ending with a **RS** row.
Shape neck
Keeping patt correct, cast off 18 (19: 19: 20: 20: 21) sts at beg of next row.
37 (38: 40: 41: 43: 43) sts.
Dec 1 st at neck edge of next 8 rows, then on foll 2 (2: 3: 3: 4: 4) alt rows, then on foll 4th row. 26 [27: 28: 29: 30: 30) sts.
Work 4 rows, ending with a WS row.
Shape shoulder
Cast off 9 (9: 9: 10: 10: 10) sts at beg of next and foll alt row.
Work 1 row.
Cast off rem 8 (9: 10: 9: 10: 10) sts.

Mark positions for 6 buttons along left front opening edge – lowest button to come 8 rows down from eyelet row, next button to come in row 3 of main textured patt, top button to come 4 rows down from start of neck shaping, and rem 3 buttons evenly spaced between 2nd and top buttons.
When working right front, make buttonholes to correspond with these button positions as folls:
Buttonhole row (RS): MP, K until there are 4 sts on right needle, K2tog tbl, (yfwd) twice (to make a buttonhole – work into front and back of this double yfwd on next row), K2tog, patt to end.
Note that no reference will be made to buttonholes within right front patt.

RIGHT FRONT
Making buttonholes as required and as given above, work as folls:
Cast on 71 (74: 78: 81: 85: 91) sts using 2 ¼ mm (US 1) needles.
Row 1 (RS): MP, K to end.
Row 2: Knit.
Rep last 2 rows 7 (7: 8: 8: 9: 9) times more, ending with a WS row.
Change to 2 ¾ mm (US 2) needles.
Next row (RS): MP, K until there are 10 sts on right needle, P to end.
Next row: Knit.
Now work in lower cluster patt as folls:
Row 1 (RS): MP, K until there are 10 sts on right needle, *P5, yon, K1, yfrn, rep from * to last 7 (4: 2: 5: 3: 3) sts, P7 (4: 2: 5: 3: 3).
Row 2: K7 (4: 2: 5: 3: 3), *P3, K5, rep from * to last 10 sts, K10.
These 2 rows set the sts – front opening edge 10 sts in g st with picot worked at beg of every RS row and rem sts in lower cluster patt as given for back.
Cont as set, dec 1 st at end of 3rd and foll 12th row.
69 (72: 76: 79: 83: 89) sts.
Work 11 rows, ending with a WS row.
Next row (dec) (RS): MP, K until there are 10 sts on right needle, (P2tog) twice, K1, (P2tog) twice, patt to last 2 sts, P2tog.
64 (67: 71: 74: 78: 84) sts.
Work 1 row, ending with a WS row.
Next row (RS): MP, K until there are 10 sts on right needle, P to end.
Next row: Knit.
Working picot at beg of every RS row, now work in g st for 7 rows, ending with a **RS** row.

Next row (eyelet row) (WS): P1 (4: 1: 4: 1: 7), (P2tog tbl, yrn, P5) 7 (7: 8: 8: 9: 9) times, P2tog tbl, yrn, P2, K10.

Work in g st with picot edging for a further 6 rows, dec 1 st at centre of last row and ending with a WS row. 63 (66: 70: 73: 77: 83) sts.

Now work in main textured patt as folls:

Row 1 (RS): MP, K to end.

Row 2: P to last 10 sts, K10.

Row 3: MP, K to end.

Row 4: P5 (2: 6: 3: 1: 1), *cluster 2, P4, rep from * to last 10 sts, K10.

These 4 rows set the sts - front opening edge 10 sts still in g st with picot worked at beg of every RS row and rem sts now in main textured patt as given for back.

Complete to match left front, rev shapings.

SLEEVES (both alike)

Cast on 66 (68: 70: 72: 74: 76) sts using 2 ¼ mm (US 1) needles.

Work in g st for 14 (14: 16: 16: 18: 18) rows, ending with a WS row.

Change to 2 ¾ mm (US 2) needles.

Now work in main textured patt as folls:

Row 1 (RS): Knit.

Row 2: Purl.

Row 3: K2, M1, K to last 2 sts, M1, K2. 68 (70: 72: 74: 76: 78) sts.

Row 4: P3 (4: 5: 6: 1: 2), cluster 2, *P4, cluster 2, rep from * to last 3 (4: 5: 6: 1: 2) sts, P3 (4: 5: 6: 1: 2).

Rows 5 to 8: As rows 1 and 2, twice.

Row 9: Knit.

Row 10: P6 (1: 2: 3: 4: 5), cluster 2, *P4, cluster 2, rep from * to last 6 (1: 2: 3: 4: 5) sts, P6 (1: 2: 3: 4: 5).

Rows 11 and 12: As rows 1 and 2.

These 12 rows set position of main textured patt and beg sleeve shaping.

Working all increases as set by row 3, cont in patt, shaping sides by inc 1 st at each end of next and every foll 10th row to 84 (82: 88: 84: 90: 88) sts, then on every foll 8th (8th: 8th: 8th: 8th: 8th) row until there are 88 (92: 94: 98: 100: 104) sts, taking inc sts into patt.

Cont straight until sleeve measures 31 (32: 33: 34: 35: 36) cm, ending with a WS row.

Shape top

Keeping patt correct, cast off 5 (6: 6: 7: 7: 9) sts at beg of next 2 rows.

78 (80: 82: 84: 86: 86) sts.

Dec 1 st at each end of next 3 rows, then on foll 2 alt rows, then on 7 foll 4th rows.

54 (56: 58: 60: 62: 62) sts.

Work 1 row, ending with a WS row.

Dec 1 st at each end of next and foll 3 (5: 5: 7: 7: 7) alt rows, then on foll 3 rows, ending with a WS row.

40 (38: 40: 38: 40: 40) sts.

Cast off 3 sts at beg of next 2 rows.

Cast off rem 34 (32: 34: 32: 34: 34) sts.

MAKING UP

Press all pieces using a warm iron over a damp cloth.

Join both shoulder seams using back stitch or mattress stitch if preferred.

Collar

Cast on 112 (116: 120: 124: 128: 132) sts using 2 ¼ mm (US 1) needles.

Work in g st for 8 (8: 8: 9: 9: 10) cm, ending with a WS row.

Cast off 10 sts at beg of next 2 rows, 5 sts at beg of foll 6 rows, then 11 sts at beg of foll 2 rows.

Cast off rem 40 (44: 48: 52: 56: 60) sts.

Sew shaped cast-off edge of collar to neck edge, placing row-end edges of collar halfway across top of front bands as in photograph.

Join side seams. Join sleeve seams.

Set sleeves into armholes.

Sew on buttons.

Cording

Cast on 3 sts using 2 ¼ mm (US 1) double-pointed needles.

Row 1 (RS): K3, *without turning slip these 3 sts to opposite end of needle and bring yarn to opposite end of work pulling it quite tightly across **WS** of work, K these 3 sts again, rep from * until cord is 140 (140: 145: 145: 150: 150)cm long.

Cast off.

Using photograph as a guide, thread cording through eyelet row at waist and tie ends at centre front.

40 (44: 47: 49: 51.5: 56) cm
15 ¾ (17 ¼: 18 ½: 19 ¼: 20 ¼: 22) in

53 (54: 55: 56: 57: 58) cm
21 (21 ¼: 22 ¾: 22: 22 ½: 22¾) in

31 (32: 33: 34: 35: 36) cm
12¼ (12½: 13: 13½: 13¾: 14¼) in

JESS

Waistcoat with an elegant drape & shawl collar

Recommendation

Suitable for the knitter with a little experience
Please see pages 20 & 21 for photographs.

	XS	S	M	L	XL	XXL	
To fit bust	81	86	91	97	102	109	cm
	32	34	36	38	40	43	in

Rowan Lenpur Linen

7 7 8 8 9 9 x 50gm

Photographed in Tattoo

Needles

1 pair 3¼mm (no 10) (US 3) needles

Tension

24 sts and 42 rows to 10 cm measured over
moss stitch using 3¼mm (US 3) needles.

BACK

Cast on 85 (91: 97: 103: 109: 119) sts using
3¼mm (US 3) needles.
Row 1 (RS): K1 (0: 1: 0: 1: 0), P1, K1, P0 (1:
0: 1: 0: 1), wrap next st (by slipping next st
on left needle onto right needle, taking yarn
to opposite side of work between needles and
then slipping same st back onto left needle –
when working back across wrapped sts, work
the wrapped st and the wrapping loop tog as
one st) and turn.
Row 2: K1 (0: 1: 0: 1: 0), P1, K1, P0 (1: 0: 1:
0: 1).
Row 3: (K1, P1) 3 (0: 3: 0: 3: 0) times, (P1,
K1) 0 (3: 0: 3: 0: 3) times, wrap next st
and turn.
Row 4: (P1, K1) 3 (0: 3: 0: 3: 0) times, (K1,
P1) 0 (3: 0: 3: 0: 3) times.
These 4 rows set position of moss st.
Keeping moss st correct throughout, cont as
folls:
Row 5: Moss st 9 (9: 9: 9: 9: 10) sts, wrap
next st and turn.
Row 6 and every foll alt row: Moss st to end.
Row 7: Moss st 13 (12: 13: 12: 12: 14) sts,
wrap next st and turn.
Row 9: Moss st 17 (16: 17: 16: 16: 18) sts,
wrap next st and turn.
Row 11: Moss st 21 (20: 21: 20: 20: 22) sts,
wrap next st and turn.
Row 13: Moss st 26 (24: 26: 24: 25: 27) sts,
wrap next st and turn.
Row 15: Moss st 32 (29: 31: 29: 30: 32) sts,
wrap next st and turn.
Row 16: Moss st to end.
Sizes S, M, L, XL and XXL only
Row 17: Moss st - (35: 37: 34: 35: 37) sts,
wrap next st and turn.
Row 18: Moss st to end.
Sizes L, XL and XXL only
Row 19: Moss st - (-: -: 40: 41: 43) sts, wrap
next st and turn.
Row 20: Moss st to end.
All sizes
These 16 (18: 18: 20: 20: 20) rows complete
shaping of right back hem edge.

Next row (RS): Moss st to end.
Now shape left back hem edge as folls:
Row 1 (WS): Moss st 3 sts, wrap next st and
turn.
Row 2: Moss st to end.
Row 3: Moss st 6 sts, wrap next st and turn.
Row 4: Moss st to end.
Now work rows 5 to 16 (18: 18: 20: 20: 20)
rows as given for shaping of right back hem
edge.
These 16 (18: 18: 20: 20: 20) rows complete
shaping of left back hem edge.
Now work 1 row in moss st across all sts
– hem shaping now complete.
Work 8 (6: 6: 6: 6: 6) rows, ending with
a WS row.
Next row (inc) (RS): Moss st 3 sts, inc twice
in next st, moss st to last 4 sts, inc twice in
next st, moss st 3 sts.
89 (95: 101: 107: 113: 123) sts.
Working all increases as set by last row, inc
2 sts at each end of 26th and foll 26th row.
97 (103: 109: 115: 121: 131) sts.
Work 21 (23: 25: 25: 27: 29) rows, ending
with a WS row.

Shape armholes

Cast off 5 (6: 7: 7: 8: 8) sts at beg of next
2 rows.
87 (91: 95: 101: 105: 115) sts.
Next row (dec) (RS): Moss st 3 sts, work
3 tog, moss st to last 6 sts, work 3 tog, moss
st 3 sts. 83 (87: 91: 97: 101: 111) sts.
Working all decreases as set by last row, dec
2 sts at each end of 4th (4th: 4th: 4th: 4th:
2nd) and 2 (2: 2: 2: 2: 4) foll 4th rows, then
on 2 (2: 2: 2: 2: 1) foll 6th rows.
63 (67: 71: 77: 81: 87) sts.
Work 33 (35: 33: 31: 31: 31) rows, ending
with a WS row.
Inc 2 sts at each end of next and 1 (1: 2: 1:
1: 1) foll 12th rows, then on 1 (1: 0: 1: 2: 2)
foll 10th rows, then on 0 (0: 0: 1: 0: 0) foll
8th row.
75 (79: 83: 93: 97: 103) sts.
Work 5 (5: 7: 5: 5: 7) rows, ending with
a WS row.

Shape back neck

Next row (RS): Moss st 23 (24: 24: 28: 29: 31) sts and turn, leaving rem sts on a holder.

Work each side of neck separately.

Dec 1 st at neck edge of next row. 22 (23: 23: 27: 28: 30) sts.

Shape shoulder

Cast off 7 (7: 7: 8: 9: 9) sts at beg and dec 1 st at end of next and foll alt row.

Work 1 row.

Cast off rem 6 (7: 7: 9: 8: 10) sts.

With RS facing, rejoin yarn to rem sts, cast off centre 29 (31: 35: 37: 39: 41) sts, moss st to end.

Complete to match first side, reversing shapings.

LEFT FRONT

Cast on 69 (72: 75: 78: 79: 85) sts using 3¼mm (US 3) needles.

Row 1 (RS): K1 (0: 1: 0: 1: 0), *P1, K1, rep from * to last 0 (0: 0: 0: 0: 1) st, P0 (0: 0: 0: 0: 1).

This row sets position of moss st.

Keeping moss st correct throughout, cont as folls:

Row 2: Moss st 5 sts, wrap next st and turn.

Row 3 and every foll alt row: Moss st to end.

Row 4: Moss st 10 sts, wrap next st and turn.

Row 6: Moss st 15 sts, wrap next st and turn.

Row 8: Moss st 20 (20: 20: 19: 19: 19) sts, wrap next st and turn.

Row 10: Moss st 25 (25: 24: 23: 23: 23) sts, wrap next st and turn.

Row 12: Moss st 29 (29: 28: 27: 27: 27) sts, wrap next st and turn.

Row 14: Moss st 33 (33: 32: 31: 31: 31) sts, wrap next st and turn.

Row 16: Moss st 37 (37: 36: 35: 35: 35) sts, wrap next st and turn.

Row 18: Moss st 41 (41: 40: 38: 39: 39) sts, wrap next st and turn.

Row 20: Moss st 44 (44: 44: 41: 42: 42) sts, wrap next st and turn.

Row 22: Moss st 47 (47: 47: 44: 45: 45) sts, wrap next st and turn.

Row 24: Moss st 50 (50: 50: 47: 48: 48) sts, wrap next st and turn.

Row 26: Moss st 53 (53: 53: 50: 51: 51) sts, wrap next st and turn.

Row 28: Moss st 56 (56: 56: 53: 54: 54) sts, wrap next st and turn.

Row 30: Moss st 59 (59: 59: 56: 57: 57) sts, wrap next st and turn.

Row 32: Moss st 61 (62: 62: 59: 60: 60) sts, wrap next st and turn.

Row 34: Moss st 63 (64: 65: 62: 63: 63) sts, wrap next st and turn.

Row 36: Moss st 65 (66: 67: 65: 66: 66) sts, wrap next st and turn.

Row 38: Moss st 67 (68: 69: 68: 69: 69) sts, wrap next st and turn.

Row 39: Moss st to end.

Sizes S, M, L, XL and XXL only

Row 40: Moss st - (70: 71: 70: 71: 72) sts, wrap next st and turn.

Row 41: Moss st to end.

Sizes M, L, XL and XXL only

Row 42: Moss st - (-: 73: 72: 73: 75) sts, wrap next st and turn.

Row 43: Moss st to end.

Sizes L, XL and XXL only

Row 44: Moss st - (-: -: 74: 75: 77) sts, wrap next st and turn.

Row 45: Moss st to end

Row 46: Moss st - (-: -: 76: 77: 79) sts, wrap next st and turn.

Row 47: Moss st to end.

Size XXL only

Row 48: Moss st 81 sts, wrap next st and turn.

Row 49: Moss st to end

Row 50: Moss st 83 sts, wrap next st and turn.

Row 51: Moss st to end.

All sizes

Next row (WS): Moss st to end.

These 40 (42: 44: 48: 48: 52) rows complete hem shaping.

Work 16 (20: 20: 20: 16: 16) rows, ending with a WS row.

Shape for shawl collar

Working all shaping as given for back, inc 2 sts at end of next and foll 8th row, then on foll 0 (0: 0: 3: 4: 4) 4th rows, then on 2 (2: 2: 0: 0: 0) foll 6th rows, then on foll 8th row **and at same time** dec 2 sts at beg of 9th (5th: 5th: 7th: 11th: 11th) row. 77 (80: 83: 88: 91: 97) sts.

Dec 2 sts at beg of 6th (2nd: 2nd: 4th: 4th: 4th) and foll 0 (26th: 26th: 26th: 26th: 26th) row. 75 (76: 79: 84: 87: 93) sts.

Work 25 (3: 3: 3: 3: 5) rows, ending with a WS row.

Shape front slope

Counting in from beg (front opening edge) of last row, place marker after 21st st.

Next row (RS): (Moss st 3 sts, work 3 tog) 1 (0: 0: 0: 0: 0) times, moss st to within 3 sts of marker, work 3 tog (for front slope dec), slip marker onto right needle, moss st 21 sts. 71 (74: 77: 82: 85: 91) sts.

Working all front slope decreases 21 sts in from front opening edge as set by last row, cont as folls:

Dec 2 sts at front slope edge of 10th (10th: 8th: 10th: 10th: 10th) and foll 10th (-: 10th: 10th: 10th: 10th) row. 67 (72: 73: 78: 81: 87) sts.

Work 1 (9: 3: 1: 3: 3) rows, ending with a WS row.

Shape armhole

Keeping moss st correct, cast off 5 (6: 7: 7: 8: 8) sts at beg and dec 0 (2: 0: 0: 0: 0) sts at front slope edge of next row. 62 (64: 66: 71: 73: 79) sts.

Work 1 row.

Dec 2 sts at armhole edge of next and foll 0 (0: 0: 0: 0: 1) alt row, then on 3 (3: 3: 3: 3: 4) foll 4th rows, then on 2 (2: 2: 2: 2: 1) foll 6th rows **and at same time** dec 2 sts at front slope edge of 7th (9th: 5th: 9th: 5th: 5th) and 1 (1: 2: 1: 2: 2) foll 10th rows. 46 (48: 48: 55: 55: 59) sts.

Dec 2 sts at front slope edge **only** on 2nd (4th: 10th: 2nd: 10th: 10th) and 2 foll 10th rows. 40 (42: 42: 49: 49: 53) sts.

Work 7 (7: 3: 9: 1: 1) rows, ending with a WS row.

Inc 2 sts at armhole edge of next and 1 (1: 2: 1: 1: 1) foll 12th rows, then on 1 (1: 0: 1: 2: 2) foll 10th rows, then on 0 (0: 0: 1: 0: 0) foll 8th row **and at same time** dec 2 sts at front slope edge of 3rd (3rd: 7th: next: 9th: 9th) and 2 (2: 1: 3: 2: 2) foll 10th rows. 40 (42: 44: 49: 51: 55) sts.

Sizes M, XL and XXL only

Dec 2 sts at front slope edge of – (-: 2nd: -: 6th: 6th) row. - (-: 42: -: 49: 53) sts.

All sizes

Work 7 (7: 7: 7: 1: 3) rows, ending with a WS row.

Shape shoulder

Cast off 7 (7: 7: 8: 9: 9) sts at beg of next and foll alt row, then 6 (7: 7: 9: 8: 10) sts at beg of foll alt row. 20 (21: 21: 24: 23: 25) sts.

Cont in moss st on these sts only (for back neck border extension) for a further 28 (30: 34: 36: 38: 40) rows, ending with a **RS** row.

Next row (WS): Moss st 14 sts, wrap next st and turn.

Next row: Moss st to end.

Next row: Moss st 7 sts, wrap next st and turn.

Next row: Moss st to end.

Cast off in moss st (on **WS**).

RIGHT FRONT

Cast on 69 (72: 75: 78: 79: 85) sts using
3¼mm (US 3) needles.

Row 1 (RS): P0 (0: 0: 0: 0: 1), (K1, P1) twice,
K1 (1: 1: 1: 1: 0), wrap next st and turn.

This row sets position of moss st.

Keeping moss st correct throughout, now work
rows 3 to 39 (41: 47: 47: 47: 51) as given for
left front.

Work 2 rows in moss st across all sts, ending
with a WS row.

These 40 (42: 44: 48: 48: 52) rows complete
hem shaping.

Work 16 (20: 20: 20: 16: 16) rows, ending
with a WS row.

Shape for shawl collar

Working all shaping as given for back, inc 2
sts at beg of next and foll 8th row, then on foll
0 (0: 0: 3: 4: 4) 4th rows, then on 2 (2: 2: 0:
0: 0) foll 6th rows, then on foll 8th row **and at
same time** dec 2 sts at end of 9th (5th: 5th:
7th: 11th: 11th) row.

77 (80: 83: 88: 91: 97) sts.

Dec 2 sts at end of 6th (2nd: 2nd: 4th: 4th:
4th) and foll 0 (26th: 26th: 26th: 26th: 26th)
row. 75 (76: 79: 84: 87: 93) sts.

Work 25 (3: 3: 3: 3: 5) rows, ending with
a WS row.

Shape front slope

Counting in from end (front opening edge)
of last row, place marker after 21st st.

Next row (RS): Moss st 21 sts, slip marker
onto right needle, work 3 tog (for front slope
dec), moss st to last 6 (0: 0: 0: 0: 0) sts, (work
3 tog, moss st 3 sts) 1 (0: 0: 0: 0: 0) times.
71 (74: 77: 82: 85: 91) sts.

Working all front slope decreases 21 sts
in from front opening edge as set by last
row, complete to match left front, reversing
shapings.

MAKING UP

Pin the pieces out and steam gently without
allowing the iron to touch the yarn.

Join both shoulder seams using back stitch or
mattress stitch if preferred. Join cast-off edges
of back neck border extensions, then sew one
edge to back neck. Join side seams.

21 (22: 22: 23: 24: 25) cm
8 ¼ (8½: 8½: 9: 9: 10) in

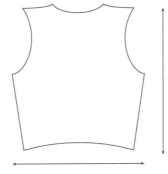

45 (46: 47: 48: 49: 50) cm
17¾ (18: 18½: 19: 19¼: 19¾) in

40.5 (43: 45.5: 48: 50.5: 54.5) cm
16 (17: 18: 19: 20: 21½) in

Recommendation

Suitable for the knitter with a little experience
Please see pages 22 & 23 for photographs.

	XS	S	M	L	XL	XXL	
To fit bust	81	86	91	97	102	109	cm
	32	34	36	38	40	43	in

Rowan Milk Cotton DK

13 14 14 15 15 16 x 50gm
Photographed in Opaque

Needles

1 pair 2¾mm (no 12) (US 2) needles
1 pair 3¼mm (no 10) (US 3) needles
Cable needle

Buttons – 3

Tension

26 sts and 36 rows to 10 cm measured over
pattern using 3¼mm (US 3) needles.

SPECIAL ABBREVIATIONS

cn = cable needle; **C6B** = slip next 3 sts onto
cn and leave at back of work, K3, then K3 from
cn; **C6F** = slip next 3 sts onto cn and leave at
front of work, K3, then K3 from cn; **C8B** = slip
next 4 sts onto cn and leave at back of work,
K4, then K4 from cn; **C8F** = slip next 4 sts
onto cn and leave at front of work, K4, then K4
from cn; **C10B** = slip next 5 sts onto cn and
leave at back of work, K5, then K5 from cn;
C10F = slip next 5 sts onto cn and leave at
front of work, K5, then K5 from cn.

SAGE

A-line cable jacket

BACK

Cast on 151 (157: 163: 171: 177: 187) sts
using 3¼mm (US 3) needles.
Row 1 (RS): P0 (0: 1: 0: 1: 0), (K1 tbl, P1) 11
(11: 12: 13: 14: 17) times, *K2tog, yfrn, P1,
(K2, inc in next st) twice, K2, P1, (K2, inc in
next st) twice, K2, P1, yon, K2tog tbl, P1, (K1
tbl, P1) 2 (3: 3: 4: 4: 4) times, rep from * twice
more, K2tog, yfrn, P1, (K2, inc in next st) twice,
K2, P1, (K2, inc in next st) twice, K2, P1, yon,
K2tog tbl, (P1, K1 tbl) 11 (11: 12: 13: 14: 17)
times, P0 (0: 1: 0: 1: 0).
167 (173: 179: 187: 193: 203) sts.
Now work in patt as folls:
Row 1 (WS): K22 (22: 25: 26: 29: 34), *P2,
K1, (P10, K1) twice, P2, K5 (7: 7: 9: 9: 9), rep
from * twice more, P2, K1, (P10, K1) twice, P2,
K22 (22: 25: 26: 29: 34).
Row 2: P0 (0: 1: 0: 1: 0), (K1 tbl, P1) 11 (11:
12: 13: 14: 17) times, *yon, K2tog tbl, (P1,
K10) twice, P1, K2tog, yfrn, P1, (K1 tbl, P1)
2 (3: 3: 4: 4: 4) times, rep from * twice more,
yon, K2tog tbl, (P1, K10) twice, P1, K2tog, yfrn,
(P1, K1 tbl) 11 (11: 12: 13: 14: 17) times,
P0 (0: 1: 0: 1: 0).
Row 3: As row 1.
Row 4: P0 (0: 1: 0: 1: 0), (K1 tbl, P1) 11 (11:
12: 13: 14: 17) times, *K2tog, yfrn, (P1, K10)
twice, P1, yon, K2tog tbl, P1, (K1 tbl, P1) 2
(3: 3: 4: 4: 4) times, rep from * twice more,
K2tog, yfrn, (P1, K10) twice, P1, yon, K2tog
tbl, (P1, K1 tbl) 11 (11: 12: 13: 14: 17)
times, P0 (0: 1: 0: 1: 0).
These 4 rows form patt.
Work in patt for a further 15 rows, ending with
a WS row.
Row 21 (RS): Patt 25 (25: 28: 29: 32: 37) sts,
*C10B, P1, C10F, patt 11 (13: 13: 15: 15: 15)
sts, rep from * twice more, C10B, P1, C10F,
patt 25 (25: 28: 29: 32: 37) sts.
Work 17 rows.
Row 39 (RS): Work 2 tog, patt 23 (23: 26: 27:
30: 35) sts, *C10B, P1, C10F, patt 11 (13: 13:
15: 15: 15) sts, rep from * twice more, C10B,
P1, C10F, patt 23 (23: 26: 27: 30: 35) sts, work
2 tog. 165 (171: 177: 185: 191: 201) sts.

Work 17 rows.
Row 57 (RS): Patt 24 (24: 27: 28: 31: 36)
sts, *slip next 5 sts onto cn and leave at back
of work, K3, K2tog, then K2tog, K3 from cn,
P1, slip next 5 sts onto cn and leave at front of
work, K3, K2tog, then K2tog, K3 from cn, patt
11 (13: 13: 15: 15: 15) sts, rep from * twice
more, slip next 5 sts onto cn and leave at back
of work, K3, K2tog, then K2tog, K3 from cn,
P1, slip next 5 sts onto cn and leave at front of
work, K3, K2tog, then K2tog, K3 from cn, patt
24 (24: 27: 28: 31: 36) sts.
149 (155: 161: 169: 175: 185) sts.
Now working 8 sts in each cable panel (instead
of 10 sts), work 15 rows.
Row 73 (RS): Work 2 tog, patt 22 (22: 25: 26:
29: 34) sts, *C8B, P1, C8F, patt 11 (13: 13:
15: 15: 15) sts, rep from * twice more, C8B,
P1, C8F, patt 22 (22: 25: 26: 29: 34) sts, work
2 tog.
147 (153: 159: 167: 173: 183) sts.
Work 15 rows.
Row 89 (RS): Patt 23 (23: 26: 27: 30: 35) sts,
*C8B, P1, C8F, patt 11 (13: 13: 15: 15: 15)
sts, rep from * twice more, C8B, P1, C8F, patt
23 (23: 26: 27: 30: 35) sts.
Work 15 rows.
Row 105 (RS): Patt 23 (23: 26: 27: 30: 35)
sts, *slip next 4 sts onto cn and leave at back
of work, K2, K2tog, then K2tog, K2 from cn,
P1, slip next 4 sts onto cn and leave at front of
work, K2, K2tog, then K2tog, K2 from cn, patt
11 (13: 13: 15: 15: 15) sts, rep from * twice
more, slip next 4 sts onto cn and leave at back
of work, K2, K2tog, then K2tog, K2 from cn,
P1, slip next 4 sts onto cn and leave at front of
work, K2, K2tog, then K2tog, K2 from cn, patt
23 (23: 26: 27: 30: 35) sts.
131 (137: 143: 151: 157: 167) sts.
Now working 6 sts in each cable panel (instead
of 8 sts), work 13 rows.
Row 119 (RS): Patt 23 (23: 26: 27: 30: 35)
sts, *C6B, P1, C6F, patt 11 (13: 13: 15: 15:
15) sts, rep from * twice more, C6B, P1, C6F,
patt 23 (23: 26: 27: 30: 35) sts.
Last 14 rows form patt for rest of back.

Work 1 (1: 5: 5: 5: 5) rows, ending with a WS row. (Back should measure 33 (33: 34: 34: 34: 34) cm.)

Shape armholes

Keeping patt correct, cast off 5 (6: 6: 7: 7: 8) sts at beg of next 2 rows. 121 (125: 131: 137: 143: 151) sts.

Dec 1 st at each end of next 7 (7: 9: 9: 11: 13) rows, then on foll 3 (4: 4: 5: 5: 6) alt rows, then on foll 4th row.

99 (101: 103: 107: 109: 111) sts.

Cont straight until armhole measures 18 (19: 19: 20: 21: 22) cm, ending with a WS row.

Shape shoulders and back neck

Cast off 8 (8: 8: 9: 9: 9) sts at beg of next 2 rows. 83 (85: 87: 89: 91: 93) sts.

Next row (RS): Cast off 8 (8: 8: 9: 9: 9) sts, patt until there are 12 (12: 13: 12: 13: 14) sts on right needle and turn, leaving rem sts on a holder.

Work each side of neck separately.

Cast off 4 sts at beg of next row.

Cast off rem 8 (8: 9: 8: 9: 10) sts.

With RS facing, rejoin yarn to rem sts, cast off centre 43 (45: 45: 47: 47: 47) sts, patt to end. Complete to match first side, reversing shapings.

LEFT FRONT

Cast on 85 (88: 91: 95: 98: 103) sts using 3¼mm (US 3) needles.

Row 1 (RS): P0 (0: 1: 0: 1: 0), (K1 tbl, P1) 11 (11: 12: 13: 14: 17) times, K2tog, yfrn, P1, (K2, inc in next st) twice, K2, P1, (K2, inc in next st) twice, K2, P1, yon, K2tog tbl, P1, (K1 tbl, P1) 2 (3: 3: 4: 4: 4) times, K2tog, yfrn, P1, (K2, inc in next st) twice, K2, P1, (K2, inc in next st) twice, K2, P1, yon, K2tog tbl, P12 (13: 13: 14: 14: 14).

93 (96: 99: 103: 106: 111) sts.

Now work in patt as folls:

Row 1 (WS): K12 (13: 13: 14: 14: 14), P2, K1, (P10, K1) twice, P2, K5 (7: 7: 9: 9: 9), P2, K1, (P10, K1) twice, P2, K22 (22: 25: 26: 29: 34).

Row 2: P0 (0: 1: 0: 1: 0), (K1 tbl, P1) 11 (11: 12: 13: 14: 17) times, yon, K2tog tbl, (P1, K10) twice, P1, K2tog, yfrn, P1, (K1 tbl, P1) 2 (3: 3: 4: 4: 4) times, yon, K2tog tbl, (P1, K10) twice, P1, K2tog, yfrn, P1, K11 (12: 12: 13: 13: 13).

Row 3: P11 (12: 12: 13: 13: 13), K1, P2, K1, (P10, K1) twice, P2, K5 (7: 7: 9: 9: 9), P2, K1, (P10, K1) twice, P2, K22 (22: 25: 26: 29: 34).

Row 4: P0 (0: 1: 0: 1: 0), (K1 tbl, P1) 11 (11: 12: 13: 14: 17) times, K2tog, yfrn, (P1, K10) twice, P1, yon, K2tog tbl, P1, (K1 tbl, P1) 2 (3: 3: 4: 4: 4) times, K2tog, yfrn, (P1, K10) twice, P1, yon, K2tog tbl, P12 (13: 13: 14: 14: 14).

These 4 rows form patt.

Work in patt for a further 15 rows, ending with a WS row.

Row 21 (RS): Patt 25 (25: 28: 29: 32: 37) sts, C10B, P1, C10F, patt 11 (13: 13: 15: 15: 15) sts, C10B, P1, C10F, patt 15 (16: 16: 17: 17: 17) sts.

Work 17 rows.

Row 39 (RS): Work 2 tog, patt 23 (23: 26: 27: 30: 35) sts, C10B, P1, C10F, patt 11 (13: 13: 15: 15: 15) sts, C10B, P1, C10F, patt 15 (16: 16: 17: 17: 17) sts.

92 (95: 98: 102: 105: 110) sts.

Work 17 rows.

Row 57 (RS): Patt 24 (24: 27: 28: 31: 36) sts, slip next 5 sts onto cn and leave at back of work, K3, K2tog, then K2tog, K3 from cn, P1, slip next 5 sts onto cn and leave at front of work, K3, K2tog, then K2tog, K3 from cn, patt 11 (13: 13: 15: 15: 15) sts, slip next 5 sts onto cn and leave at back of work, K3, K2tog, then K2tog, K3 from cn, P1, slip next 5 sts onto cn and leave at front of work, K3, K2tog, then K2tog, K3 from cn, patt 15 (16: 16: 17: 17: 17) sts. 84 (87: 90: 94: 97: 102) sts.

Now working 8 sts in each cable panel (instead of 10 sts), work 15 rows.

Row 73 (RS): Work 2 tog, patt 22 (22: 25: 26: 29: 34) sts, C8B, P1, C8F, patt 11 (13: 13: 15: 15: 15) sts, C8B, P1, C8F, patt 15 (16: 16: 17: 17: 17) sts. 83 (86: 89: 93: 96: 101) sts.

Work 15 rows.

Row 89 (RS): Patt 23 (23: 26: 27: 30: 35) sts, C8B, P1, C8F, patt 11 (13: 13: 15: 15: 15) sts, C8B, P1, C8F, patt 15 (16: 16: 17: 17: 17) sts.

Work 15 rows.

Row 105 (RS): Patt 23 (23: 26: 27: 30: 35) sts, slip next 4 sts onto cn and leave at back of work, K2, K2tog, then K2tog, K2 from cn, P1, slip next 4 sts onto cn and leave at front of work, K2, K2tog, then K2tog, K2 from cn, patt 11 (13: 13: 15: 15: 15) sts, slip next 4 sts onto cn and leave at back of work, K2, K2tog, then K2tog, K2 from cn, P1, slip next 4 sts onto cn and leave at front of work, K2, K2tog, then K2tog, K2 from cn, patt 15 (16: 16: 17: 17: 17) sts.

75 (78: 81: 85: 88: 93) sts.

Now working 6 sts in each cable panel (instead of 8 sts), work 13 rows.

Row 119 (RS): Patt 23 (23: 26: 27: 30: 35) sts, C6B, P1, C6F, patt 11 (13: 13: 15: 15: 15) sts, C6B, P1, C6F, patt 15 (16: 16: 17: 17: 17) sts.

Last 14 rows form patt for rest of left front.

Work 1 (1: 5: 5: 5: 5) rows, ending with a WS row.

Shape armhole

Keeping patt correct, cast off 5 (6: 6: 7: 7: 8) sts at beg of next row. 70 (72: 75: 78: 81: 85) sts.

Work 1 row.

Dec 1 st at armhole edge of next 7 (7: 9: 9: 11: 13) rows, then on foll 3 (4: 4: 5: 5: 6) alt rows, then on foll 4th row. 59 (60: 61: 63: 64: 65) sts.

Cont straight until 22 (22: 22: 26: 26: 26) rows less have been worked than on back to beg of shoulder shaping, ending with a WS row.

Shape neck

Next row (RS): Patt 35 (35: 36: 38: 39: 40) sts and turn, leaving rem 24 (25: 25: 25: 25: 25) sts on a holder.

Keeping patt correct, dec 1 st at neck edge of next 6 rows, then on foll 4 alt rows, then on 1 (1: 1: 2: 2: 2) foll 4th rows. 24 (24: 25: 26: 27: 28) sts.

Work 3 rows, ending with a WS row.

Shape shoulder

Cast off 8 (8: 8: 9: 9: 9) sts at beg of next and foll alt row.

Work 1 row.

Cast off rem 8 (8: 9: 8: 9: 10) sts.

Positioning buttons on patt rows 2 and 3 (the 2 K rows between the 2 P rows of the front opening edge border), mark positions for 3 buttons along front opening edge – top button to come approx 2.5 cm below neck shaping, and rem 2 buttons to come 28 rows below previous button(s).

RIGHT FRONT

Cast on 85 (88: 91: 95: 98: 103) sts using 3¼mm (US 3) needles.

Row 1 (RS): P12 (13: 13: 14: 14: 14), K2tog, yfrn, P1, (K2, inc in next st) twice, K2, P1, (K2, inc in next st) twice, K2, P1, yon, K2tog tbl, P1, (K1 tbl, P1) 2 (3: 3: 4: 4: 4) times, K2tog, yfrn, P1, (K2, inc in next st) twice, K2, P1, (K2, inc in next st) twice, K2, P1, yon, K2tog tbl, (P1, K1 tbl) 11 (11: 12: 13: 14: 17) times, P0 (0: 1: 0: 1: 0). 93 (96: 99: 103: 106: 111) sts.

Now work in patt as folls:

Row 1 (WS): K22 (22: 25: 26: 29: 34), P2, K1, (P10, K1) twice, P2, K5 (7: 7: 9: 9: 9), P2, K1, (P10, K1) twice, P2, K12 (13: 13: 14: 14: 14).

Row 2: K11 (12: 12: 13: 13: 13), P1, yon, K2tog tbl, (P1, K10) twice, P1, K2tog, yfrn, P1, (K1 tbl, P1) 2 (3: 3: 4: 4: 4) times, yon, K2tog tbl, (P1, K10) twice, P1, K2tog, yfrn, (P1, K1 tbl) 11 (11: 12: 13: 14: 17) times, P0 (0: 1: 0: 1: 0).

Row 3: K22 (22: 25: 26: 29: 34), P2, K1, (P10, K1) twice, P2, K5 (7: 7: 9: 9: 9), P2, K1, (P10, K1) twice, P2, K1, P11 (12: 12: 13: 13: 13).

Row 4: P12 (13: 13: 14: 14: 14), K2tog, yfrn, (P1, K10) twice, P1, yon, K2tog tbl, P1, (K1 tbl, P1) 2 (3: 3: 4: 4: 4) times, K2tog, yfrn, (P1, K10) twice, P1, yon, K2tog tbl, (P1, K1 tbl) 11 (11: 12: 13: 14: 17) times, P0 (0: 1: 0: 1: 0).

These 4 rows form patt.

Work in patt for a further 15 rows, ending with a WS row.

Row 21 (RS): Patt 15 (16: 16: 17: 17: 17) sts, C10B, P1, C10F, patt 11 (13: 13: 15: 15: 15) sts, C10B, P1, C10F, patt 25 (25: 28: 29: 32: 37) sts.

Work 17 rows.

Row 39 (RS): Patt 15 (16: 16: 17: 17: 17) sts, C10B, P1, C10F, patt 11 (13: 13: 15: 15: 15) sts, C10B, P1, C10F, patt 23 (23: 26: 27: 30: 35) sts, work 2 tog.

92 (95: 98: 102: 105: 110) sts.

Complete to match left front, reversing shapings, making 3 buttonholes to correspond with positions marked for buttons on left front and working first row of neck shaping as folls:

Buttonhole row 1 (RS): K4, K2tog tbl, (yfwd) twice, K2tog, patt to end.

Buttonhole row 2: Patt to double yfwd of previous row, P into front and back of double yfwd, P4.

Shape neck

Next row (RS): Patt 15 (16: 16: 17: 17: 17) sts, (K2tog) 4 times, patt 1 (1: 1: 0: 0: 0) st and slip these 20 (21: 21: 21: 21: 21) sts onto a holder, patt to end.

35 (35: 36: 38: 39: 40) sts.

SLEEVES (both alike)

Main section

Cast on 101 (105: 105: 109: 111: 115) sts using 3¼mm (US 3) needles.

Row 1 (RS): K1 tbl, *P1, K1 tbl, rep from * to end.

Row 2: Knit.

These 2 rows form patt.

Cont in patt, shaping sides by dec 1 st at each end of 5th and 7 foll 6th rows, then on foll 8th row, then on foll 10th row, then on foll 12th row, and then on foll 14th row.

77 (81: 81: 85: 87: 91) sts.

Cont straight until sleeve measures 35 (36: 37: 38: 39: 40) cm, ending with a WS row.

Shape top

Keeping patt correct, cast off 5 (6: 6: 7: 7: 8) sts at beg of next 2 rows.

67 (69: 69: 71: 73: 75) sts.

Dec 1 st at each end of next 3 rows, then on foll alt row, then on foll 4th row, then on 3 foll 6th rows, and then on 2 foll 4th rows.

47 (49: 49: 51: 53: 55) sts.

Work 1 row.

Dec 1 st at each end of next and every foll alt row to 43 sts, then on foll 7 rows, ending with a WS row.

Cast off rem 29 sts.

Cuff

With RS facing and using 2¾mm (US 2) needles, pick up and knit 101 (105: 105: 109: 111: 115) sts from cast-on edge of main section.

Row 1 (WS): K1, *sl 1, K1, psso, rep from * to end. 51 (53: 53: 55: 56: 58) sts.

Work in garter st for 7 rows, ending with a **RS** row.

Cast off knitwise (on **WS**).

MAKING UP

Pin the pieces out and steam gently without allowing the iron to touch the yarn.

Join both shoulder seams using back stitch or mattress stitch if preferred.

Neckband

With RS facing and using 2¾mm (US 2) needles, slip 20 (21: 21: 21: 21: 21) sts from right front holder onto right needle, rejoin yarn and pick up and knit 24 (24: 24: 27: 27: 27) sts up right side of neck, 39 (41: 41: 43: 43: 43) sts from back, and 24 (24: 24: 27: 27: 27) sts down left side of neck, then patt 24 (25: 25: 25: 25: 25) sts on left front holder as folls: patt 1 (1: 1: 0: 0: 0) st, (K2tog) 4 times, patt 15 (16: 16: 17: 17: 17) sts. 127 (131: 131: 139: 139: 139) sts.

Beg with a K row, work in rev st st for 4 rows, ending with a **RS** row.

Cast off knitwise (on **WS**).

Join side seams. Join sleeve seams. Insert sleeves into armholes. Sew on buttons.

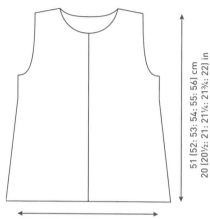

51 (52: 53: 54: 55: 56) cm
20 (20½: 21: 21¼: 21¾: 22) in

50.5 (52.5: 54.5: 58: 60.5: 64) cm
20 (50¾: 21¼: 22¾: 23¾: 25) in

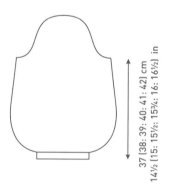

37 (38: 39: 40: 41: 42) cm
14½ (15: 15½: 15¾: 16: 16½) in

EMBRACE

Wrap cardigan

Recommendation

Suitable for the knitter with a little experience
Please see pages 24 & 25 for photographs.

	XS	S	M	L	XL	XXL	
To fit bust	**81**	**86**	**91**	**97**	**102**	**109**	**cm**
	32	34	36	38	40	43	in

Rowan Pima Cotton

	10	10	11	12	12	13 x 50gm

Photographed in Bran

Needles

1 pair 3¾mm (no 9) (US 5) needles

Tension

23 sts and 30 rows to 10 cm measured over
stocking stitch using 3¾mm (US 5) needles.

BACK

Cast on 106 (110: 116: 122: 128: 138) sts
quite loosely using 3¾mm (US 5) needles.
Row 1 (RS): K4 (4: 5: 5: 6: 7), wrap next
st (by slipping next st from left needle to
right needle, taking yarn to opposite side
of work between needles and then slipping
same st back onto left needle – when
working across wrapped sts, work the
wrapped st and the wrapping loop tog
as one st) and turn.
Row 2: Purl.
Row 3: K8 (8: 10: 10: 12: 14), wrap next st
and turn.
Row 4: Purl.
Row 5: K13 (14: 16: 17: 19: 21), wrap next
st and turn.
Row 6: Purl.
Row 7: K18 (20: 22: 24: 26: 29), wrap next
st and turn.
Row 8: Purl.
Row 9: K24 (26: 28: 31: 33: 37), wrap next
st and turn.
Row 10: Purl.
Row 11: K32 (34: 36: 39: 41: 46), wrap next
st and turn.
Row 12: Purl.
Row 13: Knit.
Row 14: P4 (4: 5: 5: 6: 7), wrap next st and
turn.
Row 15: Knit.
Row 16: P8 (8: 10: 10: 12: 14), wrap next
st and turn.
Row 17: Knit.
Row 18: P13 (14: 16: 17: 19: 21), wrap next
st and turn.
Row 19: Knit.
Row 20: P18 (20: 22: 24: 26: 28), wrap next
st and turn.
Row 21: Knit.
Row 22: P24 (26: 28: 31: 33: 37), wrap next
st and turn.
Row 23: Knit.
Row 24: P32 (34: 36: 39: 41: 46), wrap next
st and turn.
Row 25: Knit.

Row 26: Purl across **all** sts.
This completes hem shaping.
Beg with a K row, work in st st as folls:
Work 6 rows, ending with a WS row.
Next row (dec) (RS): K3, K2tog, K to last 5
sts, K2tog tbl, K3.
Working all side seam decreases as set by last
row, dec 1 st at each end of 12th and 4 foll
12th rows.
94 (98: 104: 110: 116: 126) sts.
Work 37 (37: 39: 39: 39: 39) rows, ending
with a WS row. (Back should measure 35 (35:
36: 36: 36: 36) cm at centre.)

Shape armholes

Cast off 3 (4: 4: 5: 5: 6) sts at beg of next 2
rows. 88 (90: 96: 100: 106: 114) sts.
Dec 1 st at each end of next 5 (5: 7: 7: 9: 11)
rows, then on foll 2 (2: 2: 3: 3: 4) alt rows,
then on foll 4th row.
72 (74: 76: 78: 80: 82) sts.
Cont straight until armhole measures 17 (18:
18: 19: 20: 21) cm, ending with a WS row.

Shape back neck

Next row (RS): K21 (21: 22: 22: 23: 24) and
turn, leaving rem sts on a holder.
Work each side of neck separately.
Dec 1 st at neck edge of next 2 rows. 19 (19:
20: 20: 21: 22) sts.
Work 1 row, ending with a WS row.

Shape shoulder

Cast off 6 (6: 6: 6: 6: 7) sts at beg and dec 1
st at end of next row.
Work 1 row.
Rep last 2 rows once more.
Cast off rem 5 (5: 6: 6: 7: 6) sts.
With RS facing, rejoin yarn to rem sts, cast off
centre 30 (32: 32: 34: 34: 34) sts, K to end.
Complete to match first side, reversing
shapings.

LEFT FRONT

Cast on 90 (92: 95: 98: 101: 106) sts **quite
loosely** using 3¾mm (US 5) needles.
Row 1 (RS): Knit.
Row 2: P6, wrap next st and turn.
Row 3: Knit.

Row 4: P10 (10: 10: 11: 11: 11), wrap next st and turn.

Row 5: Knit.

Row 6: P14 (14: 15: 16: 16: 16), wrap next st and turn.

Row 7: Knit.

Row 8: P18 (18: 20: 21: 21: 21), wrap next st and turn.

Row 9: Knit.

Row 10: P22 (22: 25: 26: 26: 28), wrap next st and turn.

Row 11: K to last 5 sts, K2tog tbl, K3.

Row 12: P25 (27: 30: 31: 30: 34), wrap next st and turn.

Row 13: Knit.

Row 14: P31 (33: 36: 37: 37: 41), wrap next st and turn.

Row 15: Knit.

Row 16: P37 (39: 42: 43: 44: 48), wrap next st and turn.

Row 17: As row 11.

Row 18: P42 (44: 47: 48: 50: 54), wrap next st and turn.

Row 19: Knit.

Row 20: P48 (50: 53: 56: 57: 61), wrap next st and turn.

Row 21: Knit.

Row 22: P56 (57: 61: 64: 64: 68), wrap next st and turn.

Row 23: As row 11.

Row 24: P63 (65: 68: 71: 71: 76), wrap next st and turn.

Row 25: Knit.

Row 26: P71 (73: 76: 79: 80: 85), wrap next st and turn.

Row 27: Knit.

Row 28: P79 (81: 84: 87: 89: 94), wrap next st and turn.

Row 29: As row 11.

Row 30: Purl across **all** sts.

86 (88: 91: 94: 97: 102) sts.

This completes hem shaping.

Working all side seam decreases as set by back, all front slope decreases as set by rows 11, 17, 23 and 29 and beg with a K row, now work in st st as folls:

Dec 1 st at front slope edge of 5th and 10 (12: 11: 14: 12: 11) foll 6th rows, then on 6 (4: 5: 3: 5: 5) foll 8th rows **and at same time** dec 1 st at side seam edge of 19th and 5 foll 12th rows. 63 (65: 68: 70: 73: 79) sts. Work 3 (7: 7: 5: 1: 7) rows, ending with a WS row.

Shape armhole

Cast off 3 (4: 4: 5: 5: 6) sts at beg and dec 0 (1: 1: 0: 0: 1) st at end of next row. 60 (60: 63: 65: 68: 72) sts.

Work 1 row.

Dec 1 st at armhole edge of next 5 (5: 7: 7: 9: 11) rows, then on foll 2 (2: 2: 3: 3: 4) alt rows, then on foll 4th row **and at same time** dec 1 st at front slope edge of 3rd (7th: 7th: next: 5th: 7th) and 1 (0: 1: 2: 1: 2) foll 8th rows.

50 (51: 51: 51: 53: 53) sts.

Dec 1 st at front slope edge **only** on 6th (2nd: 8th: 8th: 2nd: 8th) and 0 (1: 0: 0: 1: 0) foll 8th row, then on 2 foll 10th rows.

47 (47: 48: 48: 49: 50) sts.

Cont straight until left front matches back to start of shoulder shaping, ending with a WS row.

Shape shoulder

Cast off 6 (6: 6: 6: 6: 7) sts at beg of next and foll alt row, then 5 (5: 6: 6: 7: 6) sts at beg of foll alt row.

Cont in st st on these 30 sts only for a further 10.5 (11: 11: 11.5: 11.5: 11.5) cm, ending with a RS row.

Next row (WS): P19, wrap next st and turn.

Next row: Knit.

Next row: P9, wrap next st and turn.

Next row: Knit.

Cast off purlwise (on **WS**).

RIGHT FRONT

Cast on 90 (92: 95: 98: 101: 106) sts **quite loosely** using 3¾mm (US 5) needles.

Row 1 (RS): K6, wrap next st and turn.

Row 2 and every foll alt row: Purl.

Row 3: K10 (10: 10: 11: 11: 11), wrap next st and turn.

Row 5: K14 (14: 15: 16: 16: 16), wrap next st and turn.

Row 7: K18 (18: 20: 21: 21: 21), wrap next st and turn.

Row 9: K22 (22: 25: 26: 26: 28), wrap next st and turn.

Row 11: K3, K2tog, K21 (23: 26: 27: 25: 29), wrap next st and turn.

Row 13: K31 (33: 36: 37: 37: 41), wrap next st and turn.

Row 15: K37 (39: 42: 43: 44: 48), wrap next st and turn.

Row 17: K3, K2tog, K38 (40: 43: 44: 46: 50), wrap next st and turn.

Row 19: K48 (50: 53: 56: 57: 61), wrap next st and turn.

Row 21: K56 (57: 61: 64: 64: 68), wrap next st and turn.

Row 23: K3, K2tog, K59 (61: 64: 67: 67: 72), wrap next st and turn.

Row 25: K71 (73: 76: 79: 80: 85), wrap next st and turn.

Row 27: K79 (81: 84: 87: 89: 94), wrap next st and turn.

Row 29: K3, K2tog, K to end.

Row 30: Purl across **all** sts.

86 (88: 91: 94: 97: 102) sts.

This completes hem shaping.

Complete to match left front, reversing shapings.

SLEEVES (both alike)

Cast on 45 (45: 47: 49: 49: 51) sts using 3¾mm (US 5) needles.

Beg with a K row, now work in st st for 16 rows, ending with a WS row.

Row 17 (inc) (RS): K3, M1, K to last 3 sts, M1, K3.

Working all increases as set by last row, inc 1 st at each end of 10th (8th: 10th: 10th: 8th: 8th) and every foll 10th (8th: 10th: 10th: 8th: 8th) row to 57 (53: 65: 75: 59: 67) sts, then on every foll 12th (10th: 12th: -: 10th: 10th) row until there are 67 (71: 71: -: 77: 81) sts.

Cont straight until sleeve measures 47 (48: 49: 50: 51: 52) cm, ending with a WS row.

Shape top

Cast off 3 (4: 4: 5: 5: 6) sts at beg of next 2 rows.

61 (63: 63: 65: 67: 69) sts.

Dec 1 st at each end of next 3 rows, then on foll alt row, then on 6 foll 4th rows.

41 (43: 43: 45: 47: 49) sts.

Work 3 rows.

Dec 1 st at each end of next and foll 0 (1: 1: 2: 3: 4) alt rows, then on foll 5 rows, ending with a WS row. Cast off rem 29 sts.

Continued on next page

CLOUD
Crochet shawl

Recommendation
Suitable for the novice
Please see page 48 & 49 for photograph.

Rowan Kidsilk Aura
4 x 25gm
Photographed in Pumice

Crochet hook
9mm (no 00) (US M13) crochet hook

Tension
4 patt reps (in width) and 8 rows to 15 cm measured over pattern using 9mm (US M13) crochet hook.

Finished size
shawl measures approx 154 cm (60½ in) wide and 79 cm (31 in) at deepest point.

CROCHET ABBREVIATIONS
ch = chain; **ss** = slip stitch;
dc = double crochet; **sp(s)** = space(s);
dtr = double treble.

SHAWL
Main section
Make 166 ch using 9mm (US M13) crochet hook.

Row 1 (RS): 1 dc into 2nd ch from hook, 1 dc into each ch to end, turn. 165 sts.

Row 2: 5 ch, miss first 4 dc, 1 dc into next dc, *5 ch, miss 3 dc, 1 dc into next dc, rep from * to last 4 dc, 2 ch, miss 3 dc, 1 dtr into last dc, turn. 41 ch sps.

Row 3: 5 ch, miss first ch sp, *1 dc into next ch sp, 5 ch, rep from * until dc has been worked into last-but-one ch sp, 2 ch, 1 dtr into 3rd of 5 ch at beg of previous row, turn. 40 ch sps.
Rep last row 37 times more. 3 ch sps.

Row 41: 5 ch, miss first ch sp, 1 dc into next ch sp, 2 ch, 1 dtr into 3rd of 5 ch at beg of previous row, turn. 2 ch sps.

Row 42: 5 ch, 1 ss into 3rd of 5 ch at beg of previous row.
Fasten off.

Edging
With RS facing and using 9mm (US M13) crochet hook, attach yarn to beg of row 1 of main section, 1 ch (does NOT count as st), 1 dc into row-end edge of row 1, now work into ch sps and sts along row-end edges as folls: *1 ss into next ch sp, 1 dc into same ch sp, 3 ch, ss to 3rd ch from hook, 1 ss into same ch sp, 1 ss into next st, rep from * to end, working **3 times** into ch sp at point and replacing ss at end of last rep with 1 dc into row-end edge at end of row 1.
Fasten off.

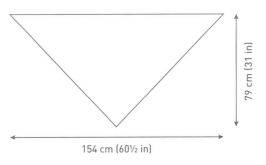

154 cm (60½ in)

79 cm (31 in)

Embrace

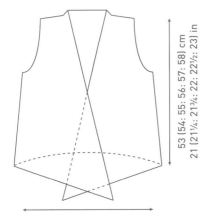

53 [54: 55: 56: 57: 58] cm
21 [21¼: 21¾: 22: 22½: 23] in

41 [42.5: 45: 48: 50.5: 55] cm
16 [16¾: 17¾ 19: 20: 20½] in

47 [48: 49: 50: 51: 52] cm
18½ [19: 19¼: 19¾: 20: 20½] in

MAKING UP
Pin the pieces out and steam gently without allowing the iron to touch the yarn.
Join both shoulder seams using back stitch or mattress stitch if preferred.
Join cast-off ends of back neck border extensions, then sew one edge to back neck.
Join side seams.
Join sleeve seams.
Insert sleeves into armholes.

LUCY

Textured jacket with covered buttons & crochet edgings

Recommendation

Suitable for the knitter with a little experience
Please see pages 28, 30 & 31 for photographs.

	XS	S	M	L	XL	XXL	
To fit bust	81	86	91	97	102	109	cm
	32	34	36	38	40	43	in

Rowan Denim

	11	12	12	13	13	14 x 50gm

Photographed in Ecru

Needles

1 pair 4mm (no 8) (US 6) needles
3.50mm (no 9) (US E4) crochet hook

Extras – 8 button frames and a pair of shoulder pads

Tension

Before washing: 22 sts and 32½ rows to 10 cm measured over pattern using 4mm (US 6) needles.

Tension note: Denim will shrink in length when washed for the first time. Allowances have been made in the pattern for shrinkage (see size diagram for after washing measurements).

CROCHET ABBREVIATIONS

ch = chain; **dc** = double crochet.

BACK

Cast on 81 (87: 93: 97: 103: 111) sts using 4mm (US 6) needles.
Next row (RS): K0 (1: 0: 0: 1: 1), *P1, K1, rep from * to last 1 (0: 1: 1: 0: 0) st, P1 (0: 1: 1: 0: 0).
Rep last row once more.
Work in patt as folls:
Row 1 (RS): K0 (1: 0: 0: 1: 1), *P1, K1, rep from * to last 1 (0: 1: 1: 0: 0) st, P1 (0: 1: 1: 0: 0).
Rows 2 to 7: As row 1.
Rows 8 and 9: P0 (1: 0: 0: 1: 1), *K1, P1, rep from * to last 1 (0: 1: 1: 0: 0) st, K1 (0: 1: 1: 0: 0).
Row 10: As row 1.
These 10 rows form patt.
Cont in patt for a further 26 rows, ending with a WS row.
Next row (RS): Patt 3 sts, work 3 tog, patt to last 6 sts, work 3 tog, patt 3 sts.
77 (83: 89: 93: 99: 107) sts.
Work 1 row.
Place markers at both ends of last row to denote top of side seam openings.
Cont in patt, dec 1 st at each end of 7th and foll 6th row.
73 (79: 85: 89: 95: 103) sts.
Work 15 rows, ending with a WS row.
Inc 1 st at each end of next and 2 foll 10th rows, then on 5 foll 8th rows, taking inc sts into patt.
89 (95: 101: 105: 111: 119) sts.
Cont straight until back measures 43.5 (43.5: 44.5: 44.5: 44.5: 44.5) cm, ending with a WS row.

Shape armholes

Keeping patt correct, cast off 3 (4: 4: 5: 5: 6) sts at beg of next 2 rows.
83 (87: 93: 95: 101: 107) sts.
Dec 1 st at each end of next 3 (3: 5: 5: 7: 7) rows, then on foll 2 (3: 3: 3: 3: 5) alt rows, then on 2 foll 4th rows.
69 (71: 73: 75: 77: 79) sts.
Cont straight until armhole measures 20 (21: 21: 22: 23.5: 24.5) cm, ending with a WS row.

Shape shoulders and back neck

Cast off 6 (6: 6: 6: 6: 7) sts at beg of next 2 rows. 57 (59: 61: 63: 65: 65) sts.
Next row (RS): Cast off 6 (6: 6: 6: 6: 7) sts, patt until there are 9 (9: 10: 10: 11: 10) sts on right needle and turn, leaving rem sts on a holder.
Work each side of neck separately.
Cast off 4 sts at beg of next row.
Cast off rem 5 (5: 6: 6: 7: 6) sts.
With RS facing, rejoin yarn to rem sts, cast off centre 27 (29: 29: 31: 31: 31) sts, patt to end.
Complete to match first side, reversing shapings.

POCKET LININGS (make 2)

Cast on 21 (21: 23: 23: 25: 25) sts using 4mm (US 6) needles.
Work in patt as folls:
Row 1 (RS): K1, *P1, K1, rep from * to end.
Rows 2 to 7: As row 1.
Rows 8 and 9: P1, *K1, P1, rep from * to end.
Row 10: As row 1.
These 10 rows form patt.
Cont in patt for a further 28 rows, ending with a WS row.
Break yarn and leave sts on a holder.

LEFT FRONT

Cast on 46 (49: 52: 54: 57: 61) sts using 4mm (US 6) needles.
Next row (RS): K0 (1: 0: 0: 1: 1), *P1, K1, rep from * to end.
Next row: *K1, P1, rep from * to last 0 (1: 0: 0: 1: 1) st, K0 (1: 0: 0: 1: 1).
Work in patt as folls:
Row 1 (RS): K0 (1: 0: 0: 1: 1), *P1, K1, rep from * to end.
Row 2: *K1, P1, rep from * to last 0 (1: 0: 0: 1: 1) st, K0 (1: 0: 0: 1: 1).
Rows 3 to 6: As rows 1 and 2.
Row 7: As row 1.
Row 8: *P1, K1, rep from * to last 0 (1: 0: 0: 1: 1) st, P0 (1: 0: 0: 1: 1).
Row 9: P0 (1: 0: 0: 1: 1), *K1, P1, rep from * to end.

Row 10: As row 2.

These 10 rows form patt.

Cont in patt for a further 26 rows, ending with a WS row.

Next row (RS): Patt 3 sts, work 3 tog, patt to end. 44 (47: 50: 52: 55: 59) sts.

Work 1 row.

Place marker at end of last row to denote top of side seam opening.

Work 9 rows, dec 1 st at beg of 7th of these rows and ending with a **RS** row.
43 (46: 49: 51: 54: 58) sts.

Place pocket

Next row (WS): Patt 16 (16: 18: 18: 20: 20) sts, cast off next 21 (21: 23: 23: 25: 25) sts in patt, patt to end.

Next row: Patt 6 (9: 8: 10: 9: 13) sts, with RS facing patt across 21 (21: 23: 23: 25: 25) sts of first pocket lining, patt to end.

Work 2 rows, dec 1 st at beg of 2nd row.
42 (45: 48: 50: 53: 57) sts.

Work 15 rows, ending with a WS row.

Inc 1 st at beg of next and 2 foll 10th rows, then on 5 foll 8th rows, taking inc sts into patt.
50 (53: 56: 58: 61: 65) sts.

Cont straight until left front matches back to beg of armhole shaping, ending with a WS row.

Shape armhole

Keeping patt correct, cast off 3 (4: 4: 5: 5: 6) sts at beg of next row. 47 (49: 52: 53: 56: 59) sts.

Work 1 row.

Dec 1 st at armhole edge of next 3 (3: 5: 5: 7: 7) rows, then on foll 2 (3: 3: 3: 3: 5) alt rows, then on 2 foll 4th rows. 40 (41: 42: 43: 44: 45) sts.

Cont straight until 23 (23: 23: 25: 25: 25) rows less have been worked than on back to beg of shoulder shaping, ending with a **RS** row.

Shape neck

Keeping patt correct, cast off 15 (16: 16: 16: 16: 16) sts at beg of next row.
25 (25: 26: 27: 28: 29) sts.

Dec 1 st at neck edge of next 4 rows, then on foll 2 (2: 2: 3: 3: 3) alt rows, then on foll 4th row, then on foll 6th row.
17 (17: 18: 18: 19: 20) sts.

Work 4 rows, ending with a WS row.

Shape shoulder

Cast off 6 (6: 6: 6: 6: 7) sts at beg of next and foll alt row.

Work 1 row.

Cast off rem 5 (5: 6: 6: 7: 6) sts.

Mark positions for 8 buttons along left front opening edge – first to come in row 41, last to come 3 cm below neck shaping, and rem 6 buttons evenly spaced between.

RIGHT FRONT

Cast on 46 (49: 52: 54: 57: 61) sts using 4mm (US 6) needles.

Next row (RS): *K1, P1, rep from * to last 0 (1: 0: 0: 1: 1) st, K0 (1: 0: 0: 1: 1).

Next row: K0 (1: 0: 0: 1: 1), *P1, K1, rep from * to end.

Work in patt as folls:

Row 1 (RS): *K1, P1, rep from * to last 0 (1: 0: 0: 1: 1) st, K0 (1: 0: 0: 1: 1).

Row 2: K0 (1: 0: 0: 1: 1), *P1, K1, rep from * to end.

Rows 3 to 6: As rows 1 and 2.

Row 7: As row 1.

Row 8: P0 (1: 0: 0: 1: 1), *K1, P1, rep from * to end.

Row 9: *P1, K1, rep from * to last 0 (1: 0: 0: 1: 1) st, P0 (1: 0: 0: 1: 1).

Row 10: As row 2.

These 10 rows form patt.

Cont in patt for a further 26 rows, ending with a WS row.

Next row (RS): Patt to last 6 sts, work 3 tog, patt 3 sts. 44 (47: 50: 52: 55: 59) sts.

Work 1 row.

Place marker at beg of last row to denote top of side seam opening.

Row 41 (buttonhole row) (RS): Patt 4 sts, work 2 tog tbl, (yrn) twice (to make a buttonhole – on next row work into front and back of this double yrn), work 2 tog, patt to end.

Making a further 7 buttonholes in this way to correspond with positions marked for buttons on left front and noting that no further reference will be made to buttonholes, cont as folls:

Work 8 rows, dec 1 st at end of 6th of these rows and ending with a **RS** row.
43 (46: 49: 51: 54: 58) sts.

Place pocket

Next row (WS): Patt 6 (9: 8: 10: 9: 13) sts, cast off next 21 (21: 23: 23: 25: 25) sts in patt, patt to end.

Next row: Patt 16 (16: 18: 18: 20: 20) sts, with RS facing patt across 21 (21: 23: 23: 25: 25) sts of second pocket lining, patt to end.

Complete to match left front, reversing shapings.

SLEEVES (both alike)

First section

Cast on 26 (26: 27: 28: 28: 29) sts using 4mm (US 6) needles.

Next row (RS): *K1, P1, rep from * to last 0 (0: 1: 0: 0: 1) st, K0 (0: 1: 0: 0: 1).

Next row: K0 (0: 1: 0: 0: 1), *P1, K1, rep from * to end.

Work in patt as folls:

Row 1 (RS): *K1, P1, rep from * to last 0 (0: 1: 0: 0: 1) st, K0 (0: 1: 0: 0: 1).

Row 2: K0 (0: 1: 0: 0: 1), *P1, K1, rep from * to end.

Rows 3 to 6: As rows 1 and 2.

Row 7: As row 1.

Row 8: P0 (0: 1: 0: 0: 1), *K1, P1, rep from * to end.

Row 9: *P1, K1, rep from * to last 0 (0: 1: 0: 0: 1) st, P0 (0: 1: 0: 0: 1).

Row 10: As row 2.

These 10 rows form patt.

Work in patt for a further 10 rows, inc 1 st at end of 5th of these rows and ending with a WS row. 27 (27: 28: 29: 29: 30) sts.

Break yarn and leave sts on a holder.

Second section

Cast on 26 (26: 27: 28: 28: 29) sts using 4mm (US 6) needles.

Next row (RS): K0 (0: 1: 0: 0: 1), *P1, K1, rep from * to end.

Next row: *K1, P1, rep from * to last 0 (0: 1: 0: 0: 1) st, K0 (0: 1: 0: 0: 1).

Work in patt as folls:

Row 1 (RS): K0 (0: 1: 0: 0: 1), *P1, K1, rep from * to end.

Row 2: *K1, P1, rep from * to last 0 (0: 1: 0: 0: 1) st, K0 (0: 1: 0: 0: 1).

Rows 3 to 6: As rows 1 and 2.

Row 7: As row 1.

Row 8: *P1, K1, rep from * to last 0 (0: 1: 0: 0: 1) st, P0 (0: 1: 0: 0: 1).

Row 9: P0 (0: 1: 0: 0: 1), *K1, P1, rep from * to end.

Row 10: As row 2.

These 10 rows form patt.

Work in patt for a further 10 rows, inc 1 st at beg of 5th of these rows and ending with a WS row. 27 (27: 28: 29: 29: 30) sts.

Join sections

Next row (RS): Patt to last st of second section, inc in last st of this section, then patt across 27 (27: 28: 29: 29: 30) sts of first section. 55 (55: 57: 59: 59: 61) sts.

Cont in patt across all sts, shaping sides by inc 1 st at each end of 12th (6th: 10th: 8th: 6th: 6th) and every foll 18th (14th: 16th: 14th: 12th: 12th) row to 63 (69: 65: 69: 63: 77) sts, then on every foll 20th (-: 18th: 16th: 14th: 14th) row until there are 65 (-: 69: 73: 75: 79) sts, taking inc sts into patt.

Cont straight until sleeve measures approx 39 (40: 41: 42: 43.5: 44.5) cm, ending after same patt row as on back to beg of armhole shaping and with a WS row.

Shape top

Keeping patt correct, cast off 3 (4: 4: 5: 5: 6) sts at beg of next 2 rows.

59 (61: 61: 63: 65: 67) sts.

Dec 1 st at each end of next 3 rows, then on foll alt row, then on foll 4th row, then on 5 foll 6th rows.

39 (41: 41: 43: 45: 47) sts.

Work 3 rows.

Dec 1 st at each end of next and every foll alt row until 33 sts rem, then on foll 3 rows, ending with a WS row.

Cast off rem 27 sts.

MAKING UP

Do **NOT** press.

Join both shoulder seams using back stitch or mattress stitch if preferred.

Edgings

With RS facing and using 3.50mm (US E4) crochet hook, attach yarn at marked point along left side seam edge of back, 1 ch (does NOT count as st), work one row of dc evenly down left side seam split edge to cast-on edge, across cast-on edge of back, then up left side seam split to marker, do NOT turn.

Now work 1 row of crab st (dc worked from left to right, instead of right to left) and fasten off. In same way and beg at marker along right front side seam, work edging around entire side seam opening, cast-on edges, front opening and neck edges of fronts and back. In same way, work edging across pocket opening cast-off edges.

In same way, work edging across sleeve cast-on edge, continuing edging up and around split in sleeve.

Wind spare yarn into a loose hank and slip this inside a lingerie laundry bag. Machine wash this hank of yarn and all pieces together before completing sewing up.

Join side seams, leaving seams open below

markers. Join sleeve seams. Insert sleeves into armholes. Sew pocket linings in place on inside. Using yarn washed with pieces, cover buttons following instructions on packet, then sew buttons in place. Insert shoulder pads.

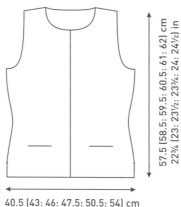

57.5 (58.5: 59.5: 60.5: 61: 62) cm
22¾ (23: 23½: 23¾: 24: 24½) in

40.5 (43: 46: 47.5: 50.5: 54) cm
16 (17: 18: 19: 20: 21¼) in

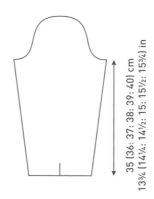

35 (36: 37: 38: 39: 40) cm
13¾ (14¼: 14½: 15: 15½: 15¾) in

Recommendation

Suitable for the knitter with a little experience
Please see pages 26 & 27 for photographs.

One size

Rowan Handknit Cotton

3 x 50gm
Photographed in Slate

Needles

1 pair 3mm (no 11) (US 2/3) needles
1 pair 4mm (no 8) (US 6) needles
Cable needle

Tension

28 sts and 30 rows to 10 cm measured over
pattern using 4mm (US 6) needles.

STARR
Cabled textured hat

HAT

Cast on 120 sts using 3mm (US 2/3) needles.
Row 1 (RS): *P1, K2, P2, (K2, P1, K2tog, yfrn,
P1) twice, K2, P2, K2, P1, rep from * 4 times
more.
Row 2: *K1, P2, K2, (P2, K1) 4 times, P2, K2,
P2, K1, rep from * 4 times more.
Row 3: *P1, K2, P2, (K2, P1, yon, K2tog tbl, P1)
twice, K2, P2, K2, P1, rep from * 4 times more.
Row 4: As row 2.
These 4 rows form fancy rib.
Work in fancy rib for a further 13 rows, ending
with a RS row.
Row 18 (inc) (WS): K1, *inc purlwise in each
of next 2 sts, K2, inc purlwise in each of next
2 sts, (K1, P2) 3 times, K1, inc purlwise in
each of next 2 sts, K2, inc purlwise in each of
next 2 sts, K2tog, rep from * 3 times more, inc
purlwise in each of next 2 sts, K2, inc purlwise
in each of next 2 sts, (K1, P2) 3 times, K1, inc
purlwise in each of next 2 sts, K2, inc purlwise
in each of next 2 sts, K1. 156 sts.
Change to 4mm (US 6) needles.
Cont in patt as folls:
Row 1 (RS): P1, *K10, P1, yon, K2tog tbl, P1,
K2, P1, yon, K2tog tbl, P1, K10, P1, rep from *
to end.
Row 2: K1, *P10, (K1, P2) 3 times, K1, P10,
K1, rep from * to end.
Row 3: P1, *K10, P1, K2tog, yfrn, P1, K2, P1,
K2tog, yfrn, P1, K10, P1, rep from * to end.
Row 4: As row 2.
Rows 5 and 6: As rows 1 and 2.
Row 7: P1, *slip next 5 sts onto cn and leave
at front of work, K5, then K5 from cn, P1,
K2tog, yfrn, P1, K2, P1, K2tog, yfrn, P1, slip
next 5 sts onto cn and leave at back of work,
K5, then K5 from cn, P1, rep from * to end.
Row 8: As row 2.
Rows 9 to 16: As rows 1 to 4, twice.
These 16 rows form patt.
Cont in patt for a further 20 rows, ending with
patt row 4 and a WS row.

Shape top

Row 1 (RS): P1, *slip next 5 sts onto cn and
leave at front of work, K3, K2tog, then K2tog,

K3 from cn, P1, K2tog tbl, P1, K2, P1, K2tog
tbl, P1, slip next 5 sts onto cn and leave at
back of work, K3, K2tog, then K2tog, K3 from
cn, P1, rep from * to end. 126 sts.
Row 2: K1, *P8, K1, P1, K1, P2, K1, P1, K1, P8,
K1, rep from * to end.
Row 3: P1, *K8, P1, K1, P1, K2, P1, K1, P1, K8,
P1, rep from * to end.
Rows 4 to 9: As rows 2 and 3, 3 times.
Row 10: As row 2.
Row 11: P1, *slip next 4 sts onto cn and leave
at front of work, K2, K2tog, then K2tog, K2
from cn, P2tog, P1, K2, P1, P2tog, slip next
4 sts onto cn and leave at back of work, K2,
K2tog, then K2tog, K2 from cn, P1, rep from *
to end. 96 sts.
Row 12: K1, *P6, K2, P2, K2, P6, K1, rep from
* to end.
Row 13: P1, *K6, P2, K2, P2, K6, P1, rep from
* to end.
Rows 14 and 15: As rows 12 and 13.
Row 16: As row 12.
Row 17: P1, *slip next 3 sts onto cn and leave
at front of work, K1, K2tog, then K2tog, K1 from
cn, P2tog, K2, P2tog, slip next 3 sts onto cn and
leave at back of work, K1, K2tog, then K2tog, K1
from cn, P1, rep from * to end. 66 sts.
Row 18: K1, *P4, K1, P2, K1, P4, K1, rep from
* to end.
Row 19: P1, *K4, P1, K2, P1, K4, P1, rep from
* to end.
Row 20: As row 18.
Row 21: P1, *(K2tog) twice, P1, K2tog, P1,
(K2tog) twice, P1, rep from * to end. 41 sts.
Row 22: K1, *P2, K1, P1, K1, P2, K1, rep from
* to end.
Row 23: P1, *K2tog tbl, slip next 2 sts onto
right needle as though to K2tog, K1, then pass
2 slipped sts over this st, K2tog, P1, rep from *
to end. 21 sts.
Break yarn and thread through rem 21 sts.
Pull up tight and fasten off securely.

MAKING UP

Join back seam, preferably using mattress
stitch.

CHALK

Relaxed belted wrap cardigan with moss stitch trim

Recommendation

Suitable for the knitter with a little experience
Please see pages 32 & 33 for photographs.

	XS	S	M	L	XL	XXL	
To fit bust	**81**	**86**	**91**	**97**	**102**	**109**	**cm**
	32	34	36	38	40	43	in

Rowan Denim

	11	12	12	13	13	14 x 50gm

Photographed in Ecru

Needles

1 pair 3¼mm (no 10) (US 3) needles
1 pair 3¾mm (no 9) (US 5) needles
1 pair 4mm (no 8) (US 6) needles

Tension

Before washing: 20 sts and 28 rows to 10 cm measured over pattern using 4mm (US 6) needles.

Tension note: Denim will shrink in length when washed for the first time. Allowances have been made in the pattern for shrinkage (see size diagram for after washing measurements).

BACK

Cast on 91 (95: 101: 105: 111: 119) sts using 3¾mm (US 5) needles.
Work in garter st for 3 rows, ending with a **RS** row.
Row 4 (WS): P0 (0: 1: 1: 0: 0), *K1, P1, rep from * to last 1 (1: 0: 0: 1: 1) st, K1 (1: 0: 0: 1: 1).
Row 5: As row 4.
Last 2 rows form moss st.
Work in moss st for a further 9 rows, ending with a WS row.
Change to 4mm (US 6) needles.
Work in patt as folls:
Row 1 (RS): Knit.
Row 2: Purl.
Rows 3 to 6: As rows 1 and 2, twice.
Row 7: K2tog, K to last 2 sts, K2tog.
89 (93: 99: 103: 109: 117) sts.
Row 8: Purl.
Row 9: Knit.
Row 10: K1 (1: 0: 0: 1: 1), *P1, K1, rep from * to last 0 (0: 1: 1: 0: 0) st, P0 (0: 1: 1: 0: 0).
Rows 11 and 12: As row 10.
These 12 rows form patt and beg side seam shaping.
Cont in patt, dec 1 st at each end of 3rd and 4 foll 8th rows, then on foll 6th row.
77 (81: 87: 91: 97: 105) sts.
Work 25 (25: 27: 27: 27: 27) rows, ending with a WS row.
Inc 1 st at each end of next and foll 8th row, then on foll 6th row, then on 2 foll 4th rows, then on foll 5 alt rows, taking inc sts into patt.
97 (101: 107: 111: 117: 125) sts.
Work 1 row, ending with a WS row.
Cast on 3 sts at beg of next 2 rows, then 6 sts at beg of next 4 rows, taking cast-on sts into patt. 127 (131: 137: 141: 147: 155) sts.
Place markers at both ends of last row to denote base of armhole openings.
Inc 1 st at each end of 13th (15th: 15th: 17th: 17th: 19th) and 2 foll 16th (16th: 16th: 16th: 18th: 18th) rows, taking inc sts into patt. 133 (137: 143: 147: 153: 161) sts.
Work 13 (15: 15: 17: 15: 17) rows, ending with a WS row. (Work should measure 21 (22: 22: 23.5: 24.5: 25.5) cm **from markers.**)

Shape shoulders and back neck

Keeping patt correct, cast off 5 (5: 6: 6: 6: 7) sts at beg of next 6 (4: 14: 14: 8: 14) rows, then 6 (6: -: -: 7: -) sts at beg of foll 8 (10: -: -: 6: -) rows.
55 (57: 59: 63: 63: 63) sts.
Next row (RS): Cast off 6 (6: 6: 7: 7: 7) sts, patt until there are 10 (10: 11: 11: 11: 11) sts on right needle and turn, leaving rem sts on a holder.
Work each side of neck separately.
Cast off 4 sts at beg of next row.
Cast off rem 6 (6: 7: 7: 7: 7) sts.
With RS facing, rejoin yarn to rem sts, cast off centre 23 (25: 25: 27: 27: 27) sts, patt to end.
Complete to match first side, rev shapings.

LEFT FRONT

Cast on 65 (67: 70: 72: 75: 79) sts using 3¾mm (US 5) needles.
Row 1 (RS): K to last 9 sts, P9.
Row 2: Knit.
Row 3: As row 1.
Row 4: P10, *K1, P1, rep from * to last 1 (1: 0: 0: 1: 1) st, K1 (1: 0: 0: 1: 1).
Row 5: P0 (0: 1: 1: 0: 0), *K1, P1, rep from * to last 9 sts, K9.
Row 6: As row 4.
Last 6 rows set the sts – front opening edge 9 sts in ridge st (6 row patt rep) with all other sts currently in moss st.
Cont as set for a further 8 rows, ending with a WS row.
Change to 4mm (US 6) needles.
Work in patt as folls:
Row 1 (RS): K to last 9 sts, patt 9 sts.
Row 2: Patt 9 sts, P to end.
Rows 3 to 6: As rows 1 and 2, twice.
Row 7: K2tog, K to last 9 sts, patt 9 sts.
64 (66: 69: 71: 74: 78) sts.
Row 8: As row 2.
Row 9: As row 1.
Row 10: Patt 9 sts, *P1, K1, rep from * to last 1 (1: 0: 0: 1: 1) st, P1 (1: 0: 0: 1: 1).
Row 11: P1 (1: 0: 0: 1: 1), *K1, P1, rep from * to last 9 sts, patt 9 sts.

Row 12: As row 10.

These 12 rows beg side seam shaping and set the sts – front opening edge 9 sts still in ridge patt with all other sts now in back as given for back.

Cont as set, dec 1 st at beg of 3rd and 4 foll 8th rows, then on foll 6th row.

58 (60: 63: 65: 68: 72) sts.

Work 13 (13: 15: 15: 15: 15) rows, ending with a WS row.

Shape front slope

Next row (RS): Patt to last 11 sts, work 2 tog tbl, patt 9 sts.

Working all front slope decreases as set by last row, dec 1 st at front slope edge of 4th and 10 foll 4th rows **and at same time** inc 1 st at beg of 12th and foll 8th row, then on foll 6th row, then on 2 foll 4th rows, then on foll 5 alt rows, taking inc sts into patt.

56 (58: 61: 63: 66: 70) sts.

Work 1 row, ending with a WS row.

Cast on 3 sts at beg of next row, then 6 sts at beg of foll 2 alt rows, taking cast-on sts into patt, **and at same time** dec 1 st at front slope edge of 3rd row. 70 (72: 75: 77: 80: 84) sts.

Work 1 row, ending with a WS row.

Place markers at end of last row to denote base of armhole opening.

Dec 1 st at front slope edge of next and 9 (10: 10: 11: 10: 8) foll 4th rows, then on 3 (3: 3: 3: 4: 6) foll 6th rows and at same time inc 1 st at beg of 13th (15th: 15th: 17th: 17th: 19th) and 2 foll 16th (16th: 16th: 16th: 18th: 18th) rows. 60 (61: 64: 65: 68: 72) sts.

Work 3 rows, ending with a WS row.

Shape shoulder

Keeping patt correct, cast off 5 (5: 6: 6: 6: 7) sts at beg of next and foll 2 (1: 7: 6: 3: 8) alt rows, then 6 (6: 7: 7: 7: -) sts at beg of foll 6 (7: 1: 2: 5: -) alt rows. 9 sts.

Work on these sts only for back neck border extension as folls:

Inc 1 st at end (shoulder cast-off edge) of next row. 10 sts.

Cont in ridge patt until border measures 8.5 (9: 9: 9.5: 9.5: 9.5) cm from last set of cast-off sts, ending with a WS row.

Cast off.

RIGHT FRONT

Cast on 65 (67: 70: 72: 75: 79) sts using 3¾mm (US 5) needles.

Row 1 (RS): P9, K to end.

Row 2: Knit.

Row 3: As row 1.

Row 4: P0 (0: 1: 1: 0: 0), *K1, P1, rep from * to last 9 sts, P9.

Row 5: K9, P1, *K1, P1, rep from * to last 1 (1: 0: 0: 1: 1) st, K1 (1: 0: 0: 1: 1).

Row 6: As row 4.

Last 6 rows set the sts – front opening edge 9 sts in ridge st (6 row patt rep) with all other sts currently in moss st.

Cont as set for a further 8 rows, ending with a WS row.

Change to 4mm (US 6) needles.

Work in patt as folls:

Row 1 (RS): Patt 9 sts, K to end.

Row 2: P to last 9 sts, patt 9 sts.

Rows 3 to 6: As rows 1 and 2, twice.

Row 7: Patt 9 sts, K to last 2 sts, K2tog. 64 (66: 69: 71: 74: 78) sts.

Row 8: As row 2.

Row 9: As row 1.

Row 10: P1 (1: 0: 0: 1: 1), *K1, P1, rep from * to last 9 sts, patt 9 sts.

Row 11: Patt 9 sts, *P1, K1, rep from * to last 1 (1: 0: 0: 1: 1) st, P1 (1: 0: 0: 1: 1).

Row 12: As row 10.

These 12 rows beg side seam shaping and set the sts – front opening edge 9 sts still in ridge patt with all other sts now in back as given for back.

Cont as set, dec 1 st at end of 3rd and 4 foll 8th rows, then on foll 6th row.

58 (60: 63: 65: 68: 72) sts.

Work 13 (13: 15: 15: 15: 15) rows, ending with a WS row.

Shape front slope

Next row (RS): Patt 9 sts, work 2 tog, patt to end.

Working all front slope decreases as set by last row, complete to match left front, rev shapings.

MAKING UP

Do NOT press.

Join both shoulder seams using back stitch or mattress stitch if preferred.

Armhole borders (both alike)

With RS facing and using 3¼mm (US 3) needles, pick up and knit 85 (89: 89: 95: 99: 103) sts evenly along armhole row-end edge between markers.

Row 1 (WS): K1, *P1, K1, rep from * to end. This row sets position of moss st.

Cont in moss st, inc 1 st at each end of 7th and foll 8th row. 89 (93: 93: 99: 103: 107) sts.

Work 8 rows, ending with a RS row.

Work in garter st for 3 rows. Cast off knitwise.

Belt

Cast on 11 sts using 3¼mm (US 3) needles.

Row 1 (RS): K3, (P1, K1) twice, P1, K3.

Row 2: As row 1.

Rep last 2 rows until belt measures 185 (190: 195: 200: 205: 210) cm, ending with a WS row. Cast off.

Machine wash all pieces together before completing sewing up.

Join cast-off edges of back neck border extensions, then sew one edge to back neck. Join side and armhole border seams, reversing seams for armhole borders. Fold armhole borders to RS as in photograph and secure in place at shoulder and side seams.

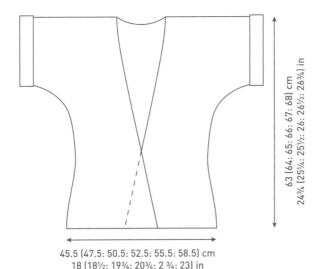

63 (64: 65: 66: 67: 68) cm
24¾ (25¼: 25½: 26: 26½: 26¾) in

45.5 (47.5: 50.5: 52.5: 55.5: 58.5) cm
18 (18½: 19¾: 20¾: 2 ¾: 23) in

DOWN
Lace & stocking stitch sweater

Recommendation
Suitable for the knitter with a little experience
Please see pages 36 & 37 for photographs.

	XS	S	M	L	XL	XXL	
To fit bust	81	86	91	97	102	109	cm
	32	34	36	38	40	43	in

Rowan Kidsilk Haze
5 6 7 7 8 8 x 25gm
Photographed in Ghost

Needles
1 pair 3¾mm (no 9) (US 5) needles
1 pair 4½mm (no 7) (US 7) needles

Tension
20 sts and 26 rows to 10 cm measured over
pattern using a combination of yarn **DOUBLE**
with 3¾mm (US 5) needles and yarn **SINGLE**
with 4½mm (US 7) needles.

BACK
Cast on 82 (86: 92: 96: 102: 110) sts using
3¾mm (US 5) needles and yarn **DOUBLE.**
Beg with a K row, work in st st for 12 (14: 6:
8: 10: 12) rows, ending with a WS row.
Now work in patt as folls:
Change to 4½mm (US 7) needles and break
off one strand of yarn.
Row 1 (RS): Using yarn **SINGLE**, (K2tog) 1
(1: 0: 0: 0: 0) times, K to last 2 (2: 0: 0: 0: 0)
sts, (K2tog) 1 (1: 0: 0: 0: 0) times. 80 (84: 92:
96: 102: 110) sts.
Rows 2 to 5: Using yarn **SINGLE**, K1, *yfwd, sl
1, K1, psso, rep from * to last st, K1.
Row 6: Using yarn **SINGLE**, purl.
Change to 3¾mm (US 5) needles and join in
2nd strand of yarn.
Row 7: Using yarn **DOUBLE**, knit.
Row 8: Using yarn **DOUBLE,** purl.
Row 9: Using yarn **DOUBLE,** (K2tog) 1 (1: 0:
0: 0: 0) times, K to last 2 (2: 0: 0: 0: 0) sts,
(K2tog) 1 (1: 0: 0: 0: 0) times.
78 (82: 92: 96: 102: 110) sts.
Row 10: Using yarn **DOUBLE**, purl.
Rows 11 and 12: As rows 7 and 8.
These 12 rows form patt and beg side seam
shaping for sizes **XS and S only.**
Cont in patt (remembering to change needles
and swap between double and single yarn as
required), dec 1 st at each end of 5th (5th:
next: next: next: next) and 2 (2: 4: 4: 4: 4) foll
8th rows. 72 (76: 82: 86: 92: 100) sts.
Work 15 rows, ending with a WS row.
Inc 1 st at each end of next and 2 foll 14th
rows, then on 2 foll 12th rows, taking inc sts
into patt. 82 (86: 92: 96: 102: 110) sts.
Work 11 (9: 9: 7: 7: 5) rows, ending after patt
row 4 (2: 2: 12: 12: 10) and with a WS row.
(Back should measure 48 (48: 49: 49:
50: 50) cm.)
Shape raglan armholes
Keeping patt correct, cast off 5 (6: 5: 6: 7: 7)
sts at beg of next 2 rows.
72 (74: 82: 84: 88: 96) sts.
Work 4 (4: 4: 4: 2: 0) rows, ending with
a WS row.

Next row (dec) (RS): K3tog, patt to last 3 sts,
K3tog tbl. 68 (70: 78: 80: 84: 92) sts.**
Working all raglan armhole decrease as set by
last row, dec 2 sts at each end of 6th (6th: 4th:
6th: 4th: 2nd) and 2 (3: 5: 5: 6: 1) foll
6th (6th: 4th: 4th: 4th: alt) rows, then on
1 (0: 0: 0: 0: 7) foll 4th rows.
52 (54: 54: 56: 56: 56) sts.
Work 3 rows, ending after patt row 12 and with
a WS row.
Cast off.

FRONT
Work as given for back to **.
Working all raglan armhole decrease as set by
last row, dec 2 sts at each end of 6th (6th: 4th:
6th: 4th: 2nd) and 2 (2: 4: 4: 5: 1) foll 6th (6th:
4th: 4th: 4th: alt) rows, then on 0 (0: 0: 0: 0: 6)
foll 4th rows. 56 (58: 58: 60: 60: 60) sts.
Work 1 (3: 1: 1: 1: 1) rows, ending with a WS row.
Shape front neck
Next row (RS): K3tog, K1 and turn, leaving
rem sts on a holder.
Work each side of neck separately.
Next row: P2tog and fasten off.
With RS facing, rejoin yarn to rem sts, cast off
centre 48 (50: 50: 52: 52: 52) sts (one st on
right needle), K3tog tbl.
Next row: P2tog and fasten off.

SLEEVES (both alike)
Cast on 40 (40: 42: 44: 44: 46) sts using
3¾mm (US 5) needles and yarn **DOUBLE.**
Beg with a K row, work in st st for 10 (14: 6:
10: 12: 6) rows, inc 0 (1: 0: 0: 0: 0) st at each
end of 13th of these rows and ending with a
WS row. 40 (42: 42: 44: 44: 46) sts.
Remembering to change needles and swap
between double and single yarn as required
and beg with patt row 1, now work in patt as
given for back, shaping sides by inc 1 st at
each end of 3rd (11th: 7th: 3rd: next: 7th)
and every foll 12th row to 44 (56: 54: 54: 64:
64) sts, then on 6 (1: 3: 4: 0: 1) foll 14th rows,
taking inc sts into patt.
56 (58: 60: 62: 64: 66) sts.

Work 13 (13: 13: 13: 11: 13) rows, ending after patt row 4 (2: 2: 12: 12: 10) and with a WS row. (Sleeve should measure 47 (48: 49: 50: 51: 52) cm.)

Shape raglan

Keeping patt correct, cast off 5 (6: 5: 6: 7: 7) sts at beg of next 2 rows.

46 (46: 50: 50: 50: 52) sts.

Work 4 rows, ending with a WS row.

Working all raglan armhole decrease as set by back, dec 2 sts at each end of next and 3 (3: 2: 3: 3: 4) foll 6th rows, then on 0 (0: 2: 1: 1: 0) foll 4th rows. 30 (30: 30: 30: 30: 32) sts.

Work 3 (5: 3: 3: 3: 3) rows, ending after patt row 8 and with a WS row.

Left sleeve only

Dec 2 sts at each end of next row, then cast off 8 (8: 8: 8: 8: 9) sts at beg of foll row. 18 (18: 18: 18: 18: 19) sts.

Work 1 row.

Cast off 8 (8: 8: 8: 8: 9) sts at beg of next row. 10 sts.

Right sleeve only

Cast off 10 (10: 10: 10: 10: 11) sts at beg and dec 2 sts at end of next row. 18 (18: 18: 18: 18: 19) sts.

Work 1 row.

Cast off 8 (8: 8: 8: 8: 9) sts at beg of next row. 10 sts.

Work 1 row.

Both sleeves

Cast off rem 10 sts.

MAKING UP

Pin the pieces out and steam gently without allowing the iron to touch the yarn.

Join both front and right back raglan seams using back stitch or mattress stitch if preferred.

Neckband

With RS facing, using 3¾mm (US 5) needles and yarn **DOUBLE,** pick up and knit 26 (26: 26: 26: 26: 28) sts from top of left sleeve, 52 (54: 54: 56: 56: 56) sts from front, 26 (26: 26: 26: 26: 28) sts from top of right sleeve, then 52 (54: 54: 56: 56: 56) sts from back. 156 (160: 160: 164: 164: 168) sts.

Row 1 (WS): Purl.

Change to 4½mm (US 7) needles and break off one strand of yarn.

Row 2: Using yarn **SINGLE,** knit.

Rows 3 to 6: Using yarn **SINGLE,** K1, *yfwd, sl 1, K1, psso, rep from * to last st, K1.

Row 7: Using yarn **SINGLE,** purl.

Change to 3¾mm (US 5) needles and join in 2nd strand of yarn.

Row 8: Using yarn **DOUBLE,** knit.

Row 9: Using yarn **DOUBLE,** purl.

Rows 10 and 11: As rows 8 and 9.

Cast off knitwise.

Join left back raglan and neckband seam. Join side and sleeve seams.

41 (43: 46: 48: 51: 55) cm
16 (17: 18: 19: 20: 21½) in

60 (61: 62: 63: 64: 65) cm
23½ (24: 24½: 24¾: 25¼: 25½) in

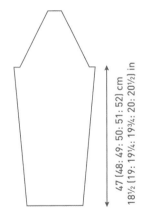

47 (48: 49: 50: 51: 52) cm
18½ (19: 19¼: 19¾: 20: 20½) in

SHIMMER
Raglan lace jacket

Recommendation

Suitable for the knitter with a little experience
Please see pages 40 & 41 for photographs.

	XS	S	M	L	XL	XXL	
To fit bust	81	86	91	97	102	109	cm
	32	34	36	38	40	43	in

Rowan Calmer

| | 7 | 8 | 8 | 9 | 9 | 10 | x 50gm |

Photographed in Cloud

Needles

1 pair 4½mm (no 7) (US 7) needles
1 pair 5mm (no 6) (US 8) needles

Buttons – 6

Tension

20 sts and 31 rows to 10 cm measured over
pattern using 5mm (US 8) needles.

Pattern note: Whilst working patt, sts are
increased on RS rows and then decreased
on the foll WS row. Count sts after WS rows
only. All st counts given do **NOT** include sts
increased on RS rows.

BACK

Cast on 86 (92: 96: 102: 106: 114) sts using
4½mm (US 7) needles.
Row 1 (RS): P0 (1: 0: 0: 0: 0), K0 (2: 1:
0: 2: 0), *P2, K2, rep from * to last 2 (1:
3: 2: 0: 2) sts, P2 (1: 2: 2: 0: 2), K0 (0:
1: 0: 0: 0).
Row 2: K0 (1: 0: 0: 0: 0), P0 (2: 1: 0: 2: 0),
*K2, P2, rep from * to last 2 (1: 3: 2: 0: 2)
sts, K2 (1: 2: 2: 0: 2), P0 (0: 1: 0: 0: 0).
These 2 rows form rib.
Work in rib for a further 10 rows, ending
with a WS row.
Change to 5mm (US 8) needles.
Now work in patt as folls:
Row 1 (RS): K3 (2: 0: 3: 1: 1), *K2, (yfwd)
twice, K2, rep from * to last 3 (2: 0: 3: 1: 1)
sts, K3 (2: 0: 3: 1: 1).
Row 2: P3 (2: 0: 3: 1: 1), *P2tog, (K1, P1)
into double yfwd of previous row, P2tog,
rep from * to last 3 (2: 0: 3: 1: 1) sts,
P3 (2: 0: 3: 1: 1).
Row 3: K1 (0: 2: 1: 3: 3), *K2, (yfwd) twice,
K2, rep from * to last 1 (0: 2: 1: 3: 3) sts, K1
(0: 2: 1: 3: 3).
Row 4: P1 (0: 2: 1: 3: 3), *P2tog, (K1, P1) into
double yfwd of previous row, P2tog, rep from *
to last 1 (0: 2: 1: 3: 3) sts, P1 (0: 2: 1: 3: 3).
These 4 rows form patt.
Cont in patt until back measures 23 (23: 24:
24: 24: 24) cm, ending with a WS row.

Shape raglan armholes

Keeping patt correct, cast off 6 sts at beg
of next 2 rows.
74 (80: 84: 90: 94: 102) sts.
Work 4 (2: 0: 0: 0: 0) rows.
Next row (RS): K2tog, patt to last 2 sts,
K2tog tbl.
Working all decreases as set by last row, dec
1 st at each end of 6th (4th: 2nd: 2nd: 2nd:
2nd) and 1 (0: 0: 0: 0: 0) foll 6th row, then on
foll 0 (0: 2: 4: 7: 13) alt rows, then
on 11 (14: 14: 14: 13: 11) foll 4th rows.
46 (48: 48: 50: 50: 50) sts.
Work 3 rows, ending with a WS row.
Cast off.

LEFT FRONT

Cast on 49 (52: 54: 57: 59: 65) sts using
4½mm (US 7) needles.
Row 1 (RS): P0 (1: 0: 0: 0: 0), K0 (2: 1: 0: 2:
0), *P2, K2, rep from * to last 9 sts, P9.
Row 2: K9, P2, *K2, P2, rep from * to last 2
(1: 3: 2: 0: 2) sts, K2 (1: 2: 2: 0: 2), P0 (0: 1:
0: 0: 0).
Row 3: P0 (1: 0: 0: 0: 0), K0 (2: 1: 0: 2: 0),
*P2, K2, rep from * to last 9 sts, K9.
Row 4: P11, *K2, P2, rep from * to last 2 (1: 3:
2: 0: 2) sts, K2 (1: 2: 2: 0: 2), P0 (0: 1: 0: 0: 0).
These 4 rows set the sts – front opening edge
9 sts in ridge patt (4 row patt rep) with all
other sts in rib.
Cont as set for a further 8 rows, inc (inc:
inc: inc: inc: dec) 1 st at end of last row and
ending with a WS row.
50 (53: 55: 58: 60: 64) sts.
Change to 5mm (US 8) needles.
Now work in patt as folls:
Row 1 (RS): K3 (2: 0: 3: 1: 1), *K2, (yfwd)
twice, K2, rep from * to last 11 sts, K2, patt 9 sts.
Row 2: Patt 9 sts, P2, *P2tog, (K1, P1) into
double yfwd of previous row, P2tog, rep from *
to last 3 (2: 0: 3: 1: 1) sts, P3 (2: 0: 3: 1: 1).
Row 3: K1 (0: 2: 1: 3: 3), *K2, (yfwd) twice, K2,
rep from * to last 13 sts, K2, yfwd, K2, patt 9 sts.
Row 4: Patt 9 sts, P3, P2tog tbl, *P2tog, (K1, P1)
into double yfwd of previous row, P2tog, rep from
* to last 1 (0: 2: 1: 3: 3) sts, P1 (0: 2: 1: 3: 3).
These 4 rows set the sts – front opening edge
9 sts still in ridge patt with all other sts now in
patt as given for back.
Cont as set until front matches back to beg of
raglan armhole shaping, ending with a WS row.

Shape raglan armhole

Keeping patt correct, cast off 6 sts at beg of
next row. 44 (47: 49: 52: 54: 58) sts.
Work 5 (3: 1: 1: 1: 1) rows.
Working all decreases as set by back, dec 1 st
at raglan armhole edge of next and 2 (0: 0: 0:
0: 0) foll 6th rows, then on foll 0 (0: 3: 5: 8:
14) alt rows, then on 8 (12: 11: 11: 10: 8) foll
4th rows. 33 (34: 34: 35: 35: 35) sts.
Work 3 (3: 3: 1: 1: 1) rows, ending with a WS row.

Shape neck

Next row (RS): (K2tog) 1 (1: 1: 0: 0: 0) times, patt 12 (12: 12: 15: 15: 15) sts and turn, leaving rem 19 (20: 20: 20: 20: 20) sts on a holder.

13 (13: 13: 15: 15: 15) sts.

Keeping patt correct, cast off 4 sts at beg of next and foll alt row **and at same time** dec 0 (0: 0: 1: 1: 1) st at raglan armhole edge of 2nd row.

5 (5: 5: 6: 6: 6) sts.

Dec 1 st at neck edge of next and foll 1 (1: 1: 2: 2: 2) alt rows **and at same time** dec 1 st at raglan armhole edge of next (next: next: 3rd: 3rd: 3rd) row.

2 sts.

Work 1 row, ending with a WS row.

Next row (RS): K2tog and fasten off.

Mark positions for 6 buttons along left front opening edge – first button to come in row 11, last button to come 3 rows above beg of neck shaping, and rem 4 buttons evenly spaced between.

RIGHT FRONT

Cast on 49 (52: 54: 57: 59: 65) sts using 4½mm (US 7) needles.

Row 1 (RS): P9, K2, *P2, K2, rep from * to last 2 (1: 3: 2: 0: 2) sts, P2 (1: 2: 2: 0: 2), K0 (0: 1: 0: 0: 0).

Row 2: K0 (1: 0: 0: 0: 0), P0 (2: 1: 0: 2: 0), *K2, P2, rep from * to last 9 sts, K9.

Row 3: K11, *P2, K2, rep from * to last 2 (1: 3: 2: 0: 2) sts, P2 (1: 2: 2: 0: 2), K0 (0: 1: 0: 0: 0).

Row 4: K0 (1: 0: 0: 0: 0), P0 (2: 1: 0: 2: 0), *K2, P2, rep from * to last 9 sts, P9.

These 4 rows set the sts – front opening edge 9 sts in ridge patt (4 row patt rep) with all other sts in rib.

Cont as set for a further 6 rows, ending with a WS row.

Row 11 (buttonhole row) (RS): Patt 3 sts, work 2 tog tbl, (yrn) twice, work 2 tog (to make a buttonhole – on next row work twice into double yrn of previous row), patt to end.

Making a further 4 buttonholes in this way to correspond with positions marked for buttons on left front and noting that no further reference will be made to buttonholes, cont as folls:

Work 1 row, inc (inc: inc: inc: inc: dec) 1 st at beg of this row and ending with a WS row.

50 (53: 55: 58: 60: 64) sts.

Change to 5mm (US 8) needles.

Now work in patt as folls:

Row 1 (RS): Patt 9 sts, K2, *K2, (yfwd) twice, K2, rep from * to last 3 (2: 0: 3: 1: 1) sts, K3 (2: 0: 3: 1: 1).

Row 2: P3 (2: 0: 3: 1: 1), *P2tog, (K1, P1) into double yfwd of previous row, P2tog, rep from * to last 11 sts, P2, patt 9 sts.

Row 3: Patt 9 sts, K2, yfwd, K2, *K2, (yfwd) twice, K2, rep from * to last 1 (0: 2: 1: 3: 3) sts, K1 (0: 2: 1: 3: 3).

Row 4: P1 (0: 2: 1: 3: 3), *P2tog, (K1, P1) into double yfwd of previous row, P2tog, rep from * to last 14 sts, P2tog, P3, patt 9 sts.

These 4 rows set the sts – front opening edge 9 sts still in ridge patt with all other sts now in patt as given for back.

Complete to match left front, reversing shapings and working first row of neck shaping as folls:

Shape neck

Next row (RS): Patt 19 (20: 20: 20: 20: 20) sts and slip these sts onto a holder, patt to last 2 (2: 2: 0: 0: 0) sts, (K2tog) 1 (1: 1: 0: 0: 0) times. 13 (13: 13: 15: 15: 15) sts.

SLEEVES (both alike)
Main section

Cast on 56 (56: 58: 60: 60: 62) sts using 5mm (US 8) needles.

Now work in patt as folls:

Row 1 (RS): K2 (2: 3: 0: 0: 1), *K2, (yfwd) twice, K2, rep from * to last 2 (2: 3: 0: 0: 1) sts, K2 (2: 3: 0: 0: 1).

Row 2: P2 (2: 3: 0: 0: 1), *P2tog, (K1, P1) into double yfwd of previous row, P2tog, rep from ˣ to last 2 (2: 3: 0: 0: 1) sts, P2 (2: 3: 0: 0: 1).

Row 3: K0 (0: 1: 2: 2: 3), *K2, (yfwd) twice, K2, rep from * to last 0 (0: 1: 2: 2: 3) sts, K0 (0: 1: 2: 2: 3).

Row 4: P0 (0: 1: 2: 2: 3), *P2tog, (K1, P1) into double yfwd of previous row, P2tog, rep from * to last 0 (0: 1: 2: 2: 3) sts, P0 (0: 1: 2: 2: 3).

These 4 rows form patt.

Cont in patt, shaping sides by inc 1 st at each end of 3rd and 6 foll 6th rows, then on 6 (5: 6: 5: 4: 3) foll 4th rows, then on foll 4 (6: 4: 6: 8: 10) alt rows, taking inc sts into patt. 90 (92: 92: 96: 98: 102) sts.

Work 1 row, ending with a WS row.

(Sleeve should measure 25 cm.)

Shape raglan

Keeping patt correct, cast off 6 sts at beg of next 2 rows. 78 (80: 80: 84: 86: 90) sts.

Working all raglan decreases as set by back raglans, dec 1 st at each end of 3rd and 4 foll 4th rows, then on every foll alt row until 28 sts rem.

Work 1 row.

Left sleeve only

Dec 1 st at each end of next row, then cast off 7 sts at beg of foll row. 19 sts.

Dec 1 st at beg of next row, then cast off 9 sts at beg of foll row.

Right sleeve only

Cast off 8 sts at beg and dec 1 st at end of next row. 19 sts.

Work 1 row.

Cast off 9 sts at beg and dec 1 st at end of next row.

Work 1 row.

Both sleeves

Cast off rem 9 sts.

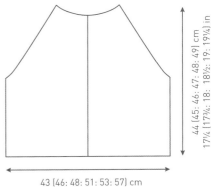

43 (46: 48: 51: 53: 57) cm
17 (18: 19: 20: 21: 22½) in

44 (45: 46: 47: 48: 49) cm
17¼ (17¾: 18: 18½: 19: 19¼) in

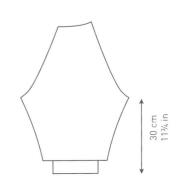

30 cm
11¾ in

Cuff

With RS facing and using 4½mm (US 7) needles, pick up and knit 42 (42: 44: 46: 46: 48) sts from cast-on edge of main section.

Row 1 (WS): K0 (0: 1: 0: 0: 1), P2, *K2, P2, rep from * to last 0 (0: 1: 0: 0: 1) st, K0 (0: 1: 0: 0: 1).

Row 2: P0 (0: 1: 0: 0: 1), K2, *P2, K2, rep from * to last 0 (0: 1: 0: 0: 1) st, P0 (0: 1: 0: 0: 1).

These 2 rows form rib.

Work in rib for a further 16 rows, ending with a **RS** row.

Cast off in rib (on **WS**).

MAKING UP

Pin the pieces out and steam gently without allowing the iron to touch the yarn.

Join all raglan seams using back stitch or mattress stitch if preferred.

Neckband

With RS facing and using 4½mm (US 7) needles, slip 19 (20: 20: 20: 20: 20) sts from right front holder onto right needle, rejoin yarn and pick up and knit 11 (11: 11: 13: 13: 13) sts up right side of neck, 26 sts from top of right sleeve, 44 (46: 46: 46: 50: 50) sts from back, 26 sts from top of left sleeve, and 11 (11: 11: 13: 13: 13) sts down left side of neck, then patt 19 (20: 20: 20: 20: 20) sts on left front holder.

156 (160: 160: 164: 168: 168) sts.

Row 1 (WS): Patt 9 sts, P2, *K2, P2, rep from * to last 9 sts, patt 9 sts.

This row sets the sts – front opening edge 9 sts still in ridge patt and all other sts in rib.

Cont as set for a further 7 rows, making 6th buttonhole in first of these rows and ending with a RS row.

Cast off in patt (on **WS**).

Join side and sleeve seams. Sew on buttons.

PEACE

Neat fitting cardigan with textured yoke detail

Recommendation

Suitable for the knitter with a little experience
Please see pages 38 & 39 for photographs.

	XS	S	M	L	XL	XXL	
To fit	81	86	91	97	102	109	cm
bust	32	34	36	38	40	43	in

Rowan Handknit cotton

9   10   11   11   12   13   x 50gm

Photographed in Raffia

Needles

1 pair 3 ¼mm (no 10) (US 3) needles
1 pair 3 ¾mm (no 9) (US 5) needles
1 pair 4mm (no 8) (US 6) needles

Buttons – 5

Tension

20 sts and 28 rows to 10cm measured over st
st using 4mm (US 6) needles

Back

Cast on 171 (183: 189: 201: 207: 225) sts
using 3 ¾ mm (US 5) needles and work lower
edging as folls:
Row 1 (RS): K3, (cast off next 3 sts, K until
3 sts on needle after 3 cast off) to end.
87 (93: 96: 102: 105: 114) sts.
Knit 1 row, dec 1 st at each end of row for
XS & S sizes, and dec 1 end of row for
M, L & XXL sizes.
85 (91: 95: 101: 105: 113) sts.
Cont in moss st, setting sts as folls:
Row 1 (RS): K0 (1: 1: 0: 0: 0), (P1, K1) to
last 1 (0: 0: 1: 1: 1) st, P1 (0: 0: 1: 1: 1).
Row 2: Work as row 1.
These 2 rows form the patt and are repeated
throughout.
Work a further 8 rows.
Next row (RS) (dec): Patt 2tog, patt until
18 (19: 21: 22: 24: 26) sts on right needle,
patt 3tog, patt to last 22 (23: 25: 26: 28: 30)
sts, patt 3tog, patt to last 2 sts, patt 2tog.
79 (85: 89: 95: 99: 107) sts.
Work 7 rows.
Next row (RS) (dec): Patt 2tog, patt until
17 (18: 20: 21: 23: 25) sts on right needle,
patt 3tog, patt to last 21 (22: 24: 25: 27: 29)
sts, patt 3tog, patt to last 2 sts, patt 2tog.
73 (79: 83: 89: 93: 101) sts.
Work 7 rows.
Next row (RS): Dec 1 st at each end of row.
71 (77: 81: 87: 91: 99) sts.
Work 5 (5: 5: 7: 7: 7) rows, ending with a WS row.
Change to 3 ¼ mm (US 3) needles.
Knit 1 row, dec 4 sts evenly over row.
67 (73: 77: 83: 87: 95) sts.
Work a further 11 (11: 13: 13: 15: 15) rows
in garter st, i.e. knit every row, ending with
a WS row.
Change to 4 mm (US 6) needles.
Beg with a K row cont in st st, shaping sides
as folls:
Work 2 rows.
Next row (RS)(Inc): K2, M1, K to last 2 sts,
M1, K2. 69 (75: 79: 85: 89: 97) sts.
Work 5 rows.

Inc as before on next row and 5 foll 8th rows.
81 (87: 91: 97: 101: 109) sts.
Work straight until back measures 21 cm from
top of garter st, ending with a WS row.
Shape armholes
Cast off 4 sts at beg of next 2 rows.
73 (79: 83: 89: 93: 101) sts
Dec 1 st at each end of next 3 (3: 3: 5: 7: 9)
rows, then on 1 (2: 3: 3: 2: 2) foll alt rows, and
then on foll 4th row.
63 (67: 69: 71: 73: 77) sts.
Work straight until armhole measures 9 cm,
ending with a **RS** row.
Now cont in garter st until armhole measures
17 (18: 19: 19: 20: 21) cm, ending with a WS row.
Shape back neck and shoulders
Next row (RS): Knit until 19 (20: 20: 21: 21:
22) sts on needle and turn, leaving rem sts on
a holder.
Work each side of neck separately.
Next row (WS) (dec): K2tog, K to end.
Next row: Cast off 5 (6: 6: 6: 6: 6) sts at beg
and dec 1 st at end of row.
Next row: K2tog, K to end.
Next row: Cast off 5 (5: 5: 6: 6: 6) sts at beg
and dec 1 st at end of row.
Knit 1 row.
Cast off rem 5 (5: 5: 5: 5: 6) sts.
With RS facing rejoin yarn to rem sts, cast off
centre 25 (27: 29: 29: 31: 33) sts, K to end.
Complete to match first side, reversing
shapings.

Left front

** Cast on 99 (105: 111: 117: 117: 129) sts
using 3 ¾ mm (US 5) needles and work lower
edging as folls:
Row 1 (RS): K3, (cast off next 3 sts, K until
3 sts on needle after 3 cast off) to end.
51 (54: 57: 60: 60: 66) sts.
Knit 1 row, dec 1 st at end of row on **XS & S**
sizes and dec 1 st in middle and one at end of
row on **M, L & XXL sizes.**
50 (53: 55: 58: 60: 64) sts. **
Cont in moss st setting sts as folls:
Row 1 (RS): K0 (1: 1: 0: 0: 0), (P1, K1) to end.

Row 2: K1, (P1, K1) 4 times, K1, (K1, P1) to last 0 (1: 1: 0: 0: 0) sts, K0 (1: 1: 0: 0: 0). These 2 rows form the pattern and set the stitches for the front band, i.e. 9 sts at centre front form the front band and are separated from the main section by 1 st of rev st st. Work a further 8 rows.

Next row (RS) (dec): Patt 2tog, patt until 18 (19: 21: 22: 24: 26) sts on right needle, patt 3tog, patt to end.
47 (50: 52: 55: 57: 61) sts.
Work 7 rows.

Next row (RS) (dec): Patt 2tog, patt until 17 (18: 20: 21: 23: 25) sts on right needle, patt 3tog, patt to end. 44 (47: 49: 52: 54: 58) sts.
Work 7 rows.

Next row (RS): Dec 1 st at beg of row.
43 (46: 48: 51: 53: 57) sts.
Work 5 (5: 5: 7: 7: 7) rows, ending with a WS row.
Change to 3 ¼ mm (US 3) needles and work in garter st across all sts.
Knit 1 row, dec 2 sts over main section.
41 (44: 46: 49: 51: 55) sts.
Work a further 11 (11: 13: 13: 15: 15) rows in garter st, i.e. knit every row, ending with a WS row.
Change to 4 mm (US 6) needles.

Next row (RS): K to last 10 sts, (P1, K1) to end.

Next row: K1, (P1, K1) 4 times, K1, P to end. These 2 row set the stitches and are repeated throughout

Next row (RS)(Inc): K2, M1, patt to end.
42 (45: 47: 50: 52: 56) sts.
Work 5 rows.
Inc 1 st as before at beg of next row and 5 foll 8th rows **and at the same time** shape front neck as folls:
Working on sts as set and keeping the side shaping correct, cont until 30 (32: 32: 32: 34: 34) rows of st st in all completed from top of garter st, ending with a WS row.

Shape front neck
Next row (RS) (dec): Keeping side shaping correct, K to last 12 sts, K2tog tbl, patt to end.
Work 3 rows.
Dec at 1 st as before at neck edge on next row and every foll 4th row and keeping side and neck shaping correct, cont until front matches back to beg of armhole shaping, ending with a WS row.

Shape armhole
Cast off 4 sts at beg of next row.
Work 1 row.
Keeping front neck shaping correct, dec 1 st at armhole edge of next 3 (3: 3: 5: 7: 9) rows, then on 1 (2: 3: 3: 2: 2) foll alt rows, and then on foll 4th row.
Cont dec 1 st as before at front edge of every 4th row until 27 (29: 30: 30: 28: 30) sts rem and then every 6th row until front matches back to start of **garter st**, ending with a RS row.
Now keeping shaping correct cont in **garter st** until 25 (26: 26: 27: 27: 28) sts rem.
Work straight until front matches back to beg of shoulder shaping, ending with a WS row.

Shape shoulder
Cast off 5 (6: 6: 6: 6: 6) sts at beg of next row and 5 (5: 5: 6: 6: 6) sts at beg of foll alt row.
Work 1 row.
Cast off 5 (5: 5: 5: 5: 6) sts at beg of next row. 10 sts.
Cont in patt for a further 8.5 (9: 9.5: 10: 10.5: 11) cm.
Cast off.
Mark position of 3 buttons, the first to come on the 5th (5th: 7th: 7th: 7th: 7th) row of garter st at waist, the 3rd 2 rows below start of neck shaping and the 2nd placed evenly between.

Right front
Work as given for left front from ** to **.
Cont in moss st setting st as folls:
Row 1 (RS): (K1, P1) to last 0 (1: 1: 0: 0: 0) st, K0 (1: 1: 0: 0: 0).
Row 2: K0 (1: 1: 0: 0: 0), (P1, K1) to last 10 sts, K1, (K1, P1) to last st, K1.
These 2 rows form the pattern and set the stitches for the front band, i.e. 9 sts at centre front form the front band and are separated from the main section by 1 st of rev st st.
Work a further 8 rows.

Next row (RS) (dec): Patt to last 22 (23: 25: 26: 28: 30) sts, patt 3 tog, patt to last 2 sts, patt 2 tog. 47 (50: 52: 55: 57: 61) sts.
Work 7 rows.

Next row (RS) (dec): Patt to last 21 (22: 24: 25: 27: 29) sts, patt 3tog, patt to last 2 sts, patt 2 tog.
44 (47: 49: 52: 54: 58) sts.
Work 7 rows.

Next row (RS): Dec 1 st at end of row.
43 (46: 48: 51: 53: 57) sts.

Work 5 (5: 5: 7: 7: 7) rows, ending with a WS row.
Change to 3 ¼ mm (US 3) needles and work in garter st across all sts.
Knit 1 row, dec 2 sts over main section.
41 (44: 46: 49: 51: 55) sts.
Work a further 3 (3: 5: 5: 5: 5) rows, ending with a WS row.

Next row (RS) (buttonhole): K4, K2tog, (yon) twice, K2tog, K to end.

Next row: Knit across row, working into back of each loop made on previous row.
Work a further 6 (6: 6: 6: 8: 8) rows in garter st, ending with a WS row.
Change to 4 mm (US 6) needles.

Next row (RS): (K1, P1) 5 times, K to end.

Next row: P to last 10 sts, K2, (P1, K1) to end.
These 2 rows set the stitches and are repeated throughout.

Next row (RS) (inc): Patt to last 2 sts, M1, K2.
42 (45: 47: 50: 52: 56) sts.
Compete to match left front, reversing shapings and working buttonholes as before to match button markers.

Left sleeve
Sleeve front
Cast on 33 (34: 35: 36: 37: 38) sts using 3 ¼ mm (US 3) needles.
Work 14 rows in garter st i.e. K every row, ending with a WS row.
Break yarn and leave sts on a spare needle.

Sleeve back
Cast on 20 (21: 22: 23: 24: 25) sts using 3 ¼ mm (US 3) needles.
Work 14 rows in garter st, ending with a WS row.
Do not break yarn.

Join sleeve front & back
Next row (RS): Working on sts for sleeve back, knit to last 6 sts, now holding sleeve back **behind** front and taking 1 st from each needle together, knit 6 sts, K to end.
47 (49: 51: 53: 55: 57) sts.
Change to 4mm (US 6) needles and, beg with a P row, cont in st st as folls:
Work 3 rows.

Next row (RS) (inc): K2, M1, K to last 2 sts, M1, K2. 49 (51: 53: 55: 57: 59) sts.
Work 9 rows.
Inc 1 st as before at each end of next row and 2 (5: 5: 5: 5: 5) foll 10th rows, and then for **XS**

size only on 3 foll 8th rows.
61 (63: 65: 67: 69: 71) sts.
Work straight until sleeve measures
31 (32: 33: 34: 35: 36) cm from cast
on edge, ending with a WS row.
Shape top
Cast off 4 sts at beg of next 2 rows.
53 (55: 57: 59: 61: 63) sts.
Dec 1 st at each end of next 3 rows,
then on foll alt row, and then on every
foll 4th row to 35 (37: 37: 41: 41: 41) sts,
ending with a **RS** row.
Work 1 row.
Dec 1 st at each end of next row and 2 (3: 2:
4: 3: 3) foll alt rows, and then on every foll row
to 23 (23: 25: 25: 27: 27) sts.
Cast off 3 sts at beg of next 2 rows.
Cast off rem 17 (17: 19: 19: 21: 21) sts.

Right sleeve
Sleeve back
Cast on 20 (21: 22: 23: 24: 25) sts using
3 ¼ mm (US 3) needles
Work 14 rows in garter st, ending with
a WS row.
Break yarn and leave sts on a spare needle.
Sleeve front
Cast on 33 (34: 35: 36: 37: 38) sts using
3 ¼ mm (US 3) needles.
Work 14 rows in garter st, ending with a WS row.
Do not break yarn.
Join sleeve back & front
Next row (RS): Working on sts for sleeve front,
knit to last 6 sts, now holding sleeve back
behind front and taking 1 st from each needle
together, knit 6 sts, K to end.
47 (49: 51: 53: 55: 57) sts.
Complete as given for left sleeve.

Making up
Press all pieces using a warm iron over
a damp cloth.
Join both shoulder seams using back stitch or
mattress stitch if preferred.
With RS facing, join cast-off edges of neck
edging together and slip stitch edging into
place along back neck.
Join side and sleeve seams.
Set sleeve top into armhole.
Press seams.
Sew on buttons.

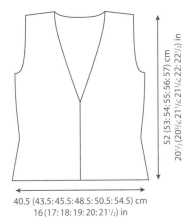

52 (53: 54: 55: 56: 57) cm
20½ (20¾: 21¼: 21¾: 22: 22½) in

40.5 (43.5: 45.5: 48.5: 50.5: 54.5) cm
16 (17: 18: 19: 20: 21½) in

31 (32: 33: 34: 35: 36) cm
12¼ (12½: 13: 13½: 13¾: 14¼) in

PETAL

Sweet sweater with texture & button trim

Recommendation

Suitable for the knitter with a little experience
Please see pages 50, 51 & 52 for photographs.

	XS	S	M	L	XL	XXL	
To fit bust	**81**	**86**	**91**	**97**	**102**	**109**	cm
	32	34	36	38	40	43	in

Rowan Fine Milk Cotton

	5	6	6	7	7	8 x 50gm

Photographed in Bloom

Needles

1 pair 2¼mm (no 13) (US 1) needles
1 pair 2¾mm (no 12) (US 2) needles
2.50mm (no 12) (US C2) crochet hook

Buttons – 12

Tension

29 sts and 38 rows to 10 cm measured over
pattern using 2¾mm (US 2) needles.

SPECIAL ABBREVIATIONS

MP = make picot as folls: cast on 1 st, then
cast off 1 st.
cluster 2 = yrn, P2, lift the yrn over these 2 sts
and off right needle.

BACK

Lower edging

Cast on 24 sts using 2¼mm (US 1) needles.
Row 1 (RS): MP, P to end.
Row 2: Knit.
Row 3: MP, K to end.
Row 4: P1, *P2tog, yrn, rep from * to last st, P1.
Rows 5 to 7: As rows 1 to 3.
Row 8: Purl.
These 8 rows form edging patt.
Rep last 8 rows 18 (19: 21: 23: 24: 26)
times more, then rows 1 to 6 again,
ending with a WS row.
Cast off but do NOT break yarn.

Upper back

With RS facing and using 2¾mm (US 2)
needles, pick up and knit 106 (114: 120:
128: 138: 146) sts evenly along straight
row-end edge of lower edging.
Next row (WS): Purl.
Now work in patt as folls:
Row 1 (RS): Knit.
Row 2: Purl.
Row 3: Knit.
Row 4: P1 (5: 2: 6: 5: 3), cluster 2, *P4,
cluster 2, rep from * to last 1 (5: 2: 6: 5: 3) sts,
P1 (5: 2: 6: 5: 3).
Rows 5 and 6: As rows 1 and 2.
Row 7: K2tog, K to last 2 sts, K2tog. 104 (112:
118: 126: 136: 144) sts.
Rows 8 and 9: As rows 2 and 3.
Row 10: P3 (1: 4: 2: 1: 5), cluster 2, *P4,
cluster 2, rep from * to last 3 (1: 4: 2: 1: 5) sts,
P3 (1: 4: 2: 1: 5).
Row 11: As row 7.
102 (110: 116: 124: 134: 142) sts.
Row 12: Purl.
These 12 rows set position of patt and start
side seam shaping.
Cont in patt, dec 1 st at each end of 3rd and
2 foll 4th rows.
96 (104: 110: 118: 128: 136) sts.
Work 13 rows, ending with a WS row.
Inc 1 st at each end of next and 8 foll 8th
rows, taking inc sts into patt.
114 (122: 128: 136: 146: 154) sts.

Cont straight until back measures 29 (29:
30: 30: 30: 30) cm from top of lower edging,
ending with a WS row.

Shape armholes

Keeping patt correct, cast off 5 (6: 6: 7: 7: 8)
sts at beg of next 2 rows.
104 (110: 116: 122: 132: 138) sts.
Dec 1 st at each end of next 5 (5: 7: 7: 9: 9)
rows, then on foll 2 (3: 2: 3: 3: 3) alt rows,
then on foll 4th row, ending with a **RS** row.
88 (92: 96: 100: 106: 112) sts.**
Cont straight until armhole measures 17 (18:
18: 19: 20: 21) cm, ending with a WS row.
Place markers at each end of 38th (40th:
40th: 42nd: 44th: 48th) row down from last
row. (These markers indicate where the front
shoulder sections start.)

Shape shoulders and back neck

Cast off 8 (8: 8: 9: 9: 10) sts at beg of next 2 rows.
72 (76: 80: 82: 88: 92) sts.
Next row (RS): Cast off 8 (8: 8: 9: 9: 10) sts,
patt until there are 11 (12: 13: 12: 14: 14) sts
on right needle and turn, leaving rem sts on a
holder.
Work each side of neck separately.
Cast off 4 sts at beg of next row.
Cast off rem 7 (8: 9: 8: 10: 10) sts.
With RS facing, rejoin yarn to rem sts, cast off
centre 34 (36: 38: 40: 42: 44) sts, patt to end.
Complete to match first side, reversing
shapings.

FRONT

Work as given for back to **.
Cast off all sts purlwise (on **WS**).

Left shoulder section

Cast on 1 st using 2¾mm (US 2) needles.
Working in st st, beg with a K row, and then in
patt as set by back from marked point upwards
when there are sufficient sts, cont as folls:
Row 1 (RS): Inc in st. 2 sts.
Row 2: Inc purlwise in first st, patt to end. 3 sts.
Work 1 row.
Row 4: Inc purlwise in first st, patt to end.
Row 5: Patt to last st, inc in last st.
Work 1 row.

Row 7: As row 5. 6 sts.
Rep rows 2 to 7, 0 (0: 0: 0: 1: 1) times more,
then rows 2 to 6, 0 (0: 1: 1: 1: 1) times more,
taking inc sts into patt.
6 (6: 9: 9: 13: 13) sts.
Work 1 (1: 0: 0: 0: 0) row, ending with a WS row.
Inc 1 st at shaped edge of next and foll 14 (15:
13: 14: 12: 14) alt rows.
21 (22: 23: 24: 26: 28) sts.
Work 1 row, ending with a WS row.

Shape shoulder
Cast off 8 (8: 8: 9: 9: 10) sts at beg and inc
1 st at end of next row.
14 (15: 16: 16: 18: 19) sts.
Work 1 row.
Rep last 2 rows once more.
Cast off rem 7 (8: 9: 8: 10: 10) sts.

Right shoulder section
Cast on 1 st using 2¾mm (US 2) needles.
Working in st st, beg with a K row, and then
in patt as set by back from marked point
upwards when there are sufficient sts,
cont as folls:
Row 1 (RS): Inc in st. 2 sts.
Row 2: Patt to last st, inc purlwise in last st. 3 sts.
Work 1 row.
Row 4: Patt to last st, inc purlwise in last st.
Row 5: Inc in first st, patt to end.
Work 1 row.
Row 7: As row 5. 6 sts.
Complete to match left shoulder section,
reversing shapings.

SLEEVES (both alike)
Lower edging (worked in 2 pieces)
**Cast on 8 sts using 2¼mm (US 1) needles.
Rep the 8 edging patt rows as given for
lower edging of back 7 (7: 7: 8: 8: 8)
times, then rows 1 to 6 again, ending
with a WS row.**
Cast off.
Rep from ** to ** once more (to make second
piece).
Cast off but do NOT break yarn.

Upper sleeve
With RS facing and using 2¾mm (US 2)
needles, pick up and knit 40 (42: 44: 45: 47:
48) sts evenly along straight row-end edge of
second lower edging piece, then 40 (42: 44:
45: 47: 48) sts evenly along straight row-end
edge of first lower edging piece.
80 (84: 88: 90: 94: 96) sts.
Next row (WS): Purl.

Now work in patt as folls:
Row 1 (RS): Knit.
Row 2: Purl.
Row 3: Knit.
Row 4: P6 (2: 4: 5: 1: 2), cluster 2, *P4,
cluster 2, rep from * to last 6 (2: 4: 5: 1: 2) sts,
P6 (2: 4: 5: 1: 2).
These 4 rows set position of patt as given
for back.
Cont in patt as now set for a further 2 (2: 4:
4: 6: 6) rows, ending with a WS row.

Shape top
Keeping patt correct, cast off 5 (6: 6: 7: 7: 8)
sts at beg of next 2 rows.
70 (72: 76: 76: 80: 80) sts.
Dec 1 st at each end of next 3 rows, then
on foll alt row, then on 5 (5: 5: 6: 6: 8) foll
4th rows.
52 (54: 58: 56: 60: 56) sts.
Work 1 row, ending with a WS row.
Dec 1 st at each end of next and foll 3 (6: 5:
6: 7: 5) alt rows, then on foll 7 (5: 7: 5: 5: 5)
rows, ending with a WS row.
30 (30: 32: 32: 34: 34) sts.
Cast off 4 sts at beg of next 2 rows.
Cast off rem 22 (22: 24: 24: 26: 26) sts.

MAKING UP
Press all pieces using a warm iron over
a damp cloth.
Join both front shoulder sections to back
along shoulder seams using back stitch
or mattress stitch if preferred.
Front neck trim
With RS facing and using 2¼mm (US 1)
needles, pick up and knit 90 (94: 98: 102:
106: 114) sts across front cast-off edge.
Row 1 (WS): P2, *K2, P2, rep from * to end.
Row 2: K2, *P2, K2, rep from * to end.
These 2 rows form rib.
Work in rib for a further 10 rows, ending
with a RS row.
Cast off in rib (on **WS**).
Front shoulder section and back neck trim
With RS facing and using 2¼mm (US 1)
needles, starting and ending at cast-on points
of front shoulder sections, pick up and knit
38 (39: 40: 43: 44: 49) sts up shaped
row-end edge of right front shoulder section,
42 (44: 46: 48: 50: 52) sts from back, then
38 (39: 40: 43: 44: 49) sts down shaped
row-end edge of left front shoulder section.
118 (122: 126: 134: 138: 150) sts.

Beg with row 1, work in rib as given for front
neck trim, inc 1 st at each end of 2nd and foll
10 rows, taking inc sts into rib.
140 (144: 148: 156: 160: 172) sts.
Cast off in rib (on **WS**).
Lay front shoulder sections over front so that
row-end edges of neck trims match and with
pick-up rows matching cast-off edges as in
photograph. Sew row-end edges together
along armhole edges. Join side seams, leaving
seams open along edges of lower edgings. Join
sleeve seams. Set sleeves into armholes.
Using 2.50mm (US C2) crochet hook, make 5
button loops along front edges of lower edging
and one button loop along front edge of sleeve
lower edging. Sew on buttons to correspond
with button loops.

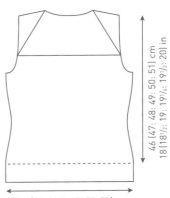

39.5 (42: 44.5: 47: 50: 53) cm
15½ (16½: 17½: 18½: 19½: 21) in

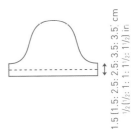

INFORMATION

A guide to assist with techniques & finishing touches

TENSION

Achieving the correct tension has to be one of the most important elements in producing a beautiful, well fitting knitted garment. The tension controls the size and shape of your finished piece and any variation to either stitches or rows, however slight, will affect your work and change the fit completely.

To avoid any disappointment, we would always recommend that you knit a tension square in the yarn and stitch given in the pattern, working perhaps four or five more stitches and rows than those given in the tension note.

When counting the tension, place your knitting on a flat surface and mark out a 10cm square with pins. Count the stitches between the pins. If you have too many stitches to 10cm your knitting it too tight, try again using thicker needles, if you have too few stitches to 10cm your knitting is too loose, so try again using finer needles. Please note, if you are unable to achieve the correct stitches and rows required, the stitches are more crucial as many patterns are knitted to length.

Keep an eye on your tension during knitting, especially if you're going back to work which has been put to one side for any length of time.

SIZING

The instructions are given for the smallest size. Where they vary, work the figures in brackets for the larger sizes. One set of figures refers to all sizes. The size diagram with each pattern will help you decide which size to knit. The measurements given on the size diagram are the actual size your garment should be when completed.

Measurements will vary from design to design because the necessary ease allowances have been made in each pattern to give your garment the correct fit, i.e. a loose fitting

garment will be several cm wider than a neat fitted one, a snug fitting garment may have no ease at all.

WORKING A LACE PATTERN

When working a lace pattern it is important to remember that if you are unable to work a full repeat i.e. both the increase and corresponding decrease and vice versa, the stitches should be worked in stocking stitch or an alternative stitch suggested in the pattern.

CHART NOTE

Some of our patterns include a chart. Each square on a chart represent a stitch and each line of squares a row of knitting.

When working from a chart, unless otherwise stated, read odd rows (RS) from right to left and even rows (WS) from left to right. The key alongside each chart indicates how each stitch is worked.

FINISHING INSTRUCTIONS

It is the pressing and finishing which will transform your knitted pieces into a garment to be proud of.

Pressing

Darn in ends neatly along the selvage edge. Follow closely any special instructions given on the pattern or ball band and always take great care not to over press your work.

Block out your knitting on a pressing or ironing board, easing into shape, and unless otherwise states, press each piece using a warm iron over a damp cloth.

Tip: Attention should be given to ribs/edgings; if the garment is close fitting – steam the ribs gently so that the stitches fill out but stay elastic. Alternatively if the garment is to hang straight then steam out to the correct shape.

Tip: Take special care to press the selvages, as this will make sewing up both easier and neater.

CONSTRUCTION
Stitching together

When stitching the pieces together, remember to match areas of pattern very carefully where they meet. Use a stitch such as back stitch or mattress stitch for all main knitting seams and join all ribs and neckband with mattress stitch, unless otherwise stated.

Take extra care when stitching the edgings and collars around the back neck of a garment. They control the width of the back neck, and if too wide the garment will be ill fitting and drop off the shoulder. Knit back neck edgings only to the length stated in the pattern, even stretching it slightly if for example, you are working in garter or horizontal rib stitch.

Stitch edgings/collars firmly into place using a back stitch seam, easing-in the back neck to fit the collar/edging rather than stretching the collar/edging to fit the back neck.

Set-in sleeves: Join side and sleeve seams. Place centre of cast off edge of sleeve to shoulder seams. Set in sleeve, easing sleeve head into armhole.

CARE INSTRUCTIONS
Yarns

Follow the care instructions printed on each individual ball band. Where different yarns are used in the same garment, follow the care instructions for the more delicate one.

Buttons

We recommend that buttons are removed if your garment is to be machine washed.

CROCHET

We are aware that crochet terminology varies from country to country. Please note we have used the English style in this publication.

Crochet abbreviations

ch	chain
ss	slip stitch
dc	double crochet
htr	half treble
tr	treble
dtr	double treble
htr2tog	half treble 2tog
tr2tog	treble 2tog
yoh	yarn over hook
sp(s)	space(s)

Double crochet

1 Insert the hook into the work (as indicated in the pattern), wrap the yarn over the hook and draw the yarn through the work only.
2 Wrap the yarn again and draw the yarn through both loops on the hook.
3 1 dc made

Half treble

1 Wrap the yarn over the hook & insert the hook into the work (as indicated in pattern).
2 Wrap the yarn over the hook draw through the work only and wrap the yarn again.
3 Draw through all 3 loops on the hook.
4 1 half treble made.

Treble

1 Wrap the yarn over the hook and insert the hook into the work (as indicated on the pattern).
2 Wrap the yarn over the hook draw through the work only and wrap the yarn again.
3 Draw through the first 2 loops only and wrap the yarn again.
4 Draw through the last 2 loops on the hook.
5 1 treble made.

ABBREVIATIONS

K	knit
P	purl
K1b	knit 1 through back loop
st(s)	stitch(es)
inc	increas(e)(ing)
dec	decreas(e)(ing)
st st	stocking stitch (1 row K, 1 row P)
garter st	garter stitch (K every row)
beg	begin(ning)
foll	following
rem	remain(ing)
rev st st	reverse stocking stitch (1 row P, 1 row K)
rep	repeat
alt	alternate
cont	continue
patt	pattern
tog	together
mm	millimetres
cm	centimetres
in(s)	inch(es)
RS	right side
WS	wrong side
sl 1	slip one stitch
psso	pass slipped stitch over
tbl	through back of loop
M1	make one stitch by picking up horizontal loop before next stitch and knitting into back of it
M1p	make one stitch by picking up horizontal loop before next stitch and purling into back of it
yfwd	yarn forward
yon	yarn over needle
yrn	yarn round needle
MP	Make picot: Cast on 1 st, by inserting the right needle between the first and second stitch on left needle, take yarn round needle, bring loop through and place on left (one stitch cast on), cast off 1 st, by knitting first the loop and then the next stitch, pass the first stitch over the second (one stitch cast off).
Cn	cable needle
C4B	Cable 4 back: Slip next 2 sts onto a cn and hold at back of work, K2, K2 from cn.
C4F	Cable 4 front: Slip next 2 sts onto a cn and hold at front of work, K2, K2 from cn.

THANK YOU

As always, to our fabulous team;
Graham, Angela, Diana, Hannah, Ann,
Lindsay, Sue, Tricia, Susan, Ella,
Sandra, Arna, Betty, Joan & Glennis.

We couldn't have done it
without each & every one of you.

INDEX